THE PEOPLE WHO
INSPIRED THE WORDS
WE USE EVERY DAY

HARVEY WALLBANGERS AND TAM O'SHANTERS

A BOOK OF EPONYMS

MARTIN HANNAN

JOHN BLAKE

Published by Metro Publishing
an imprint of John Blake Publishing Ltd
3 Bramber Court, 2 Bramber Road,
London W14 9PB, England

www.johnblakepublishing.co.uk

www.facebook.com/Johnblakepub facebook
twitter.com/johnblakepub twitter

First published in hardback in 2011

ISBN: 978 1 84358 416 2

British Library Cataloguing-in-Publication Data:

A catalogue record for this book is available from the British Library.

Design by www.envydesign.co.uk

Printed and bound by CPI Group (UK) Ltd, Croydon, CR0 4YY

1 3 5 7 9 10 8 6 4 2

Papers used by John Blake Publishing are natural, recyclable
products made from wood grown in sustainable forests.
The manufacturing processes conform to the environmental
regulations of the country of origin.

Dedication

*To the memory of my friend Dennis O'Hare,
who would have appreciated the humour.
RIP*

ACKNOWLEDGEMENTS

My thanks go to Michelle Signore and all at John Blake Publishing; my agent Mark Stanton; the staff of The Scotsman Publications library; the staff at the British Library, the National Library of Scotland, Central and Moredun Libraries in Edinburgh, and the Mitchell Library in Glasgow.

My greatest debt of gratitude goes to my wife and children for putting up with my absences when in writing mode, and my moods when not absent, and also to my mother for the use of the office (again) and her love and support these last 52 years.

CONTENTS

CONTENTS

PREFACE

Admit it – you have no real idea who Tam O'Shanter or Harvey Wallbanger were. But you're interested enough to have got this far – so read on and prepare to be entertained and enlightened in equal measure.

The fact that we mark people's achievements is a very human activity. Other species have kings and queens, pack leaders and stand-out individuals, but they are not commemorated in stone, ink or through oral history. Only the human race idolises its own.

There are statues and paintings of famous and not-so-famous people all over the world. Politicians and pop stars sometimes have airports named after them, while local worthies across the globe will be granted the honour of being forever remembered by having a street named after them. Sports stars will perhaps lend their name to a stadium, while royalty will be commemorated on the sides of ships or in the titles of charities.

Yet, for a comparatively few people, there is an honour, deserved or otherwise, which is much more lasting and can often become part of day-to-day language. Put simply, their name becomes all or part of an eponym. When it happens, for good or ill, that person gains a form of immortality, for their entry into common usage will be recorded in dictionaries and lexicons.

Eponyms are words which gain their meaning from a name, usually that of a person. They occur in most languages, but English is very good at nurturing them. Due mainly to its supremacy in science, business and worldwide culture, the English language is global, vibrant and living. It is constantly being reinvented and developed by absorption from myriad sources across the planet.

Since 'modern' English was first structured in the Middle Ages, words from different languages have been imported and adapted over the centuries, and have vastly enriched English. Human invention has also changed the language – neologisms (newly coined words or phrases) happen all the time in a fast-moving, developing world, although some die out very quickly.

Eponyms, however, stand apart. They are a word form which relies on a name, whether that name comes from a real person such as an inventor or discoverer, or from a fictional, legendary or mythical character. They are widespread and, consequently, one of the commonest phrases in modern usage is 'the eponymous ...' We usually know what 'the eponymous' means – that an item, or a quality, described either by a phrase or single word, has been given the name of some person, real or fictitious.

It seems simple – Churchillian means 'like Winston Churchill', while the Ali Shuffle or Fosbury Flop, for instance, get their names from the great sportsmen who invented these manoeuvres. A Harvey Wallbanger may – or may not – have been named after a surfer called Harvey who downed several of the cocktails and started bashing into the walls of a bar in Los Angeles; more of that later. A Tam O'Shanter also gets its name from a chap who had drunk too much, a character created by Scotland's greatest poet, Robert Burns.

Simple, yes, but the eponym is one of the most fascinating and complex instances of how language, and especially the English language, gains new words. The extraordinary evolution of English over the centuries has been the subject of many books and, in every book, the story of English is never less than complex. This book will be no different – to understand eponyms, very often you have to know or learn about subjects ranging from medieval Christianity to 20th-century cooking. That's because eponyms have a history all of their own, although few people champion them because they are so much part of our everyday usage of the language. Which is a pity, because there are marvellous stories lurking behind virtually every single one of them.

The aim of this book is to gather as many of those stories as possible. As well as examining the phenomenon that is the eponym, this book will show how they developed in English usage and changed the language in doing so. What's more, we'll have some fun along the way, because language is never less than dynamic and often endlessly surprising.

Eponyms have staying power; precious few people know

anything about Niccolo Machiavelli of Florence who died in 1527 but, nearly five centuries later, we all understand 'machiavellian' to describe a cynical and opportunistic philosophy. It is used ever more frequently in these mendacious days, but the word was already in use before the man himself died.

New eponyms crop up constantly but, like so many neologisms, they should be given no real credence unless they are still in use, say a decade later. That is why, in *Harvey Wallbangers and Tam O'Shanters*, in all but a few exceptional circumstances, the 'cut-off' date for coining will be 2001 as any eponyms minted after that date are still too young.

I will not differentiate, as some grammarians do, between so called 'true' and 'pseudo' eponyms. The former is usually seen as a word in which the original 'name' has been replaced by an understanding that has a life of its own – 'boycott' or 'hooliganism', for example.

'Pseudo-eponyms' are usually taken to be names applied to objects or ideas, such as Reaganomics or Thatcherism, or to scientific and medical terms such as Parkinson's Disease. These eponyms are just as deserving of consideration as the 'true' eponym, and the main difference appears to be whether lexicologists give an eponym an initial letter that is upper or lower case – a form of snobbery, a word which itself is arguably an eponym drawn from WM Thackeray's *Book of Snobs*. Nevertheless, almost all company names, advertising and branding eponyms – e.g. the Winalot dog, the Emirates Stadium – will be omitted, if only on grounds of good taste.

Some forms of eponym can also derive from the names of places or things, but this book concentrates on eponyms that gain their definition from people, be they real or fictional – after all, a fictional character can make for a very interesting story. That's why I have also included a small section on 'place-name' eponyms, principally because of the stories behind them.

Not every known eponym will be included. There are just too many, especially in the scientific field. *The Book of Medical Eponyms*, for instance, would have thousands of entries alone.

My collection will feature only the better known of the scientific eponyms, but the list will still be long and wide-ranging, with the main criterion – though not rigidly so – being that the eponym is already in a dictionary or encyclopaedia, dozens of which I have consulted.

In some cases, I will also show that the common presumption that a word is an eponym is simply at odds with the facts.

This book will no doubt be accused of being idiosyncratic and quirky – well, so was Samuel Johnson's *Dictionary of the English Language*. For instance, just like the good doctor, my definitions will be as long or as short as I want to make them, depending on the quality of the story behind the word.

I will also include my own eponym: Hannan's Law – the assertion that a statement has less credibility the more exaggeratedly someone states it. For instance, if someone says something is 'definite fact', you must automatically presume the 'fact' needs double-checking. Or if a politician says 'it is true to say …' then you can bet your wages on the rest of the sentence being a lie. Murphy's Law – there will be a section on these eponymous laws – unfortunately suggests that somebody else will have already coined an eponym for my Hannanist creed, but my name will go on it … and, according to Stigler's Law, someone else will supplant my name.

Harvey Wallbanger and Tam O'Shanters – A Book of Eponyms hopes to be a work that can be read for pleasure and yet will stand as a reference book for writers and all who want to enrich their language and knowledge.

It is because this book is aimed at writers and people who love using the English language that I have decided to group eponyms under headings which indicate how the word can be used, inspired by the eponymous thesaurus of Monsieur Roget. There is a full alphabetical listing at the back of the book, however.

Above all, I want to tell stories about words, and hopefully with sufficient humour to retain your interest. I view this as a work in progress and, with a website starting the week the book is published – www.martinhannan.com – I hope readers will take the chance to correct any mistakes I have made or add more eponyms and explanations.

Consequently, *Harvey Wallbangers and Tam O'Shanters – A Book of Eponyms* will not be *stentorian* in tone, but will be as light as a *zephyr*. It will not plough the *Stygian* depths of the language for every example of an eponym, and the tone will be more *Dickensian* than *Dylanesque* or *Joycean*. Nevertheless, the author's approach to this *herculean* task will be *Stakhanovite* with a touch of *Taylorist* efficiency thrown in.

See what I mean about eponyms? They're everywhere.

· 1 ·

HEROES AND VILLAINS – DEFINING QUALITIES

These eponyms are qualitative adjectives which describe attributes or features supposedly resembling those of the person, or that person's creations, whose name thus became eponymous.

ALEXANDRINE

When the word Alexandrine is used in a historical context, it refers to the era and perhaps the conquered territories of King Alexander the Great of Macedon (356–323BC). In grammar, however, 'alexandrine' has a specific use, referring to a form of verse that first emerged in France in the early Middle Ages. It is basically a line of 12 syllables with the stress on both the sixth and last syllables, and was the major verse form before William Shakespeare and others popularised the iambic pentameter.

Most scholars think Alexandrine derives from the 12th-century French chivalric romances about King Alexander the Great who famously conquered most of the known world before dying at the age of 32. These long works, some of which are attributed to the poet Alexander of Paris or Bernay, are rendered in the verse form that was later named 'alexandrine' in acknowledgement of their influence.

ARTHURIAN

Most eponyms take their root from a real person or someone in fiction, but very few derive from a person who may have been a myth, but was certainly a legend. Did King Arthur live? Do we care? He is such a hero that we want him to have lived.

When we use the word Arthurian, it is almost always in conjunction with the word legend and, as such, King Arthur might well have been a real person around whom much imaginative folklore has been weaved.

That a 'King of the Britons' of this name – and we cannot even be sure that Arthur was his name – existed on the west coast of Great Britain sometime between the 4th and 7th centuries is generally accepted by most people, except a lot of pesky historians and archaeologists who insist there is no evidence for Arthur.

How dare they! The fact is we want to believe in Camelot, its king and his sword Excalibur, his wizard Merlin and his queen Guinevere, and the knights of the Round Table. In Britain, we need an explanation why the Dark Ages of conquest and battle fell upon the whole island, and we need to believe there was a Camelot which represented a last stand of goodness against the incoming barbarism – or else why should we believe that Britain is ever going to return to that idyllic state?

The fact is that the Welsh cleric Geoffrey of Monmouth

probably invented most of the history of Arthur in his book *Historia Regum Britannia* in the 12th century. Even back then, his critics accused Geoffrey of making up most of the Arthurian tales, though they waited until after he died around 1155AD, as it was not the done thing to criticise a bishop of the Church. Invention or not, Geoffrey did us all a favour, not least because he added stories of Leir and Cymbeline which provided William Shakespeare with inspiration for his plays.

The Arthur stories grew apace after Geoffrey, with Lancelot and the Holy Grail being added by the French writer Chretien de Troyes, and then in came the Arthurian daddy of them all, Sir Thomas Malory, who penned *Le Morte d'Arthur* in the 15th century. It all adds to the legend that we are not even sure who Malory was, but he gathered all the English and French stories into one volume which still stands as the key work of Arthurian literature. Since then there have been many more Arthurian stories, and film and television works abound, which is largely why we all understand what the eponym 'Arthurian' stands for – anything to do with Camelot and its King.

AUGUSTAN

Though he was born Gaius Octavius Thurinus, the first true Emperor of Rome is better known to posterity as Augustus (63BC–14AD). What is perhaps not always realised about a man who really did change the world is that he had different names at different times during his lifetime.

Known as Octavius as a boy, he took the name Gaius Julius Caesar in honour of the great-uncle who had adopted him – history (and Shakespeare) refer to him at that time as Octavian or Octavianus. Only after he became Emperor was he awarded the name Augustus – 'Revered One' – by the Senate and, confusingly, he was also known as Caesar and referred to in Greek as Sebastos.

He finished as Augustus, however, having avenged the murder of his great-uncle Julius by beating Brutus and Cassius in battle, seeing off his former co-leaders Mark Antony and Marcus Lepidus, and reigning over Rome for 40 years in an era of relative peace and prosperity that was known as the Pax Romana. His many other reforms of the State and general control of the Republic boosted Rome's fortunes and saw him awarded divine status after his death. The Roman Empire he effectively founded lasted for centuries, but was never perhaps so glorious than in the original Augustan age.

Though the word is not as common as before, we still use 'Augustan' to refer to the best of something, the height of quality or the inspirational foundation, as in the Augustan age of English literature in the early 18th century.

BACCHANALIAN
(*See **Dionysian** below*)

BAROQUE
The trouble with history is that it is written by historians, sometimes long after events have taken place. People lose context, and fail to understand why something happened; for instance, why a word was coined at the time.

'Baroque' is usually taken to derive from a Portuguese word

'*barocco*' which supposedly meant a misshapen pearl. The connection was presumably because Baroque Christian art was so gross and over the top – out of proportion – in response to the Reformation. The Italian for Baroque is indeed '*barocco*'.

There is an alternative derivation. Federico Barocci (1526–1612) is curiously not bracketed with the very greatest of Italian artists, but it is often forgotten that his prolific work was hugely influential in the late 16th and early 17th centuries. There is a noticeable difference between his early work and his later output, after he had become a lay monk and eagerly embraced the Roman Church's struggle against the forces of the Protestant Reformation. From being an almost mainstream Renaissance artist, he became a purveyor of massively colourful art and a master painter at that period in Italy, especially Rome, which is the acknowledged forerunner of Baroque. Peter Paul Rubens was just one of the many artists influenced by Barocci.

The point is that Barocci was not his real name. He was born Federico Fiori da Urbino and was given the nickname Il Barocco, a two-wheeled cart drawn by oxen – why, we do not know – from which came Barocci. Given his fame at the start of the period we now call Baroque, is it not more likely that those he influenced acknowledged the inspiration of Il Barocco?

BLIMPISH

We call an old, set-in-his-ways fuddy-duddy a 'blimpish' character, and this is a possibly unique example of an eponym that was adopted from an existing name and then reinvented to mean something else entirely.

A blimp is a non-rigid airship, the term first being used in 1915 and supposedly deriving from the noise that was made when someone pushed a finger into the dirigible's surface. Try poking a balloon and you'll see why.

When cartoonist David Low of the *Evening Standard* was looking to satirise the British officer class of the 1930s, he created Colonel Blimp, borrowing the name from the 'gasbag' airship. Blimp was old-fashioned, fiercely reactionary and, as Low himself said, 'a symbol of stupidity'.

The wonderful British film *The Life and Death of Colonel Blimp* by Michael Powell and Emeric Pressburger made a 'blimp' slightly more sympathetic, but Winston Churchill still wanted it banned because it showed older officers as frankly doddery. The public lapped it up, however, as they loved Low's cartoons, and 'blimpish' took root and is used to describe someone who is out of touch.

BOSWELLIAN
(*n. Boswell, Boswellism*)

Dr Samuel Johnson's obsessive admirer James Boswell (1740–95) has given us an eponym which is so apt for our age of bloggers who never miss a detail of the lives of celebrities.

It is thanks to this Scottish lawyer and minor aristocrat, the 9th Laird of Auchinleck, that we know so much about Dr Samuel Johnson whose dictionary is the forerunner of all books which try to delineate the English language – including this one.

His early diaries of his travels in Europe were notable in themselves, but his life of Johnson (1791) and the brilliant journal, *Tour to the Hebrides*, saw Boswell at his very best, the book being a template for both travel writing and celebrity gossip memoirs. Despite the fact that, by his own admission, he shipped an ocean of booze in his life, Boswell remained a fastidious diarist and wrote of his encounters with famous people and prostitutes alike.

'Boswellian' has thus come to describe an obsessive chronicler and fan of another, when it could just as easily mean excessively lustful or practically alcoholic.

BYRONIC

The most common meaning of Byronic is to describe somebody that is both heroic and flawed, much like Lord George Gordon Byron (1788–1824) himself.

The 6th Baron Byron could hardly have been anything other than 'mad, bad and dangerous to know', as he was famously described by his lover Lady Caroline Lamb, not least because he was the son of 'Mad Jack' Byron, was born with his right foot clubbed, and endured an 'interesting' childhood which involved seduction by his governess at the age of ten, the same age as he inherited the barony of Byron.

He became the first and, some would say, greatest of the Romantic poets who bestrode English literature in the early 19th century. Many decades before an anti-hero was even defined, Byron created a 'hero' very much based on himself in *Childe Harolde's Pilgrimage*, his semi-autobiographical narrative poem that took him six years to complete. In the poem, Byron depicted himself as clever, arrogant, sexually louche, cynical, moody but always brave. Similar tragic and tortured heroes appeared in several more of Byron's poems and his play *Manfred*. Byronic heroes littered novels and poems from then on, and their traits can still be seen in our modern anti-hero.

There is no doubting Byron's personal courage, as he embraced unpopular political causes and played a leading role in the Greek independence campaign, though he died before seeing battle. Nor can his 'mad' traits be discounted, so this eponym is definitely accurate.

CADMEAN

(*See also* **Pyrrhic** *below*)

A word that is underused because 'Pyrrhic' is overused, 'cadmean' is exclusively seen in connection with a victory, for it means a win achieved at great loss to oneself and one's companions or entourage. Cadmus, the mythical founder of the city of Thebes, needed water for his new metropolis, and sent his followers and friends to fetch the waters from a spring. Unfortunately for them, the spring was guarded by a water dragon who made mincemeat of Cadmus's people, but not the leader himself. Having killed the monster, only then did Cadmus find out it was a pet dragon of the god Ares, who duly made his life hell on earth thereafter. Winning isn't everything, especially when you're up against the vengeful denizens of Olympus.

CAROLINGIAN

Meaning 'descended from Charles', this adjective refers to the powerful dynasty of the Frankish kings who ruled much of France and Germany from 751AD to just before the end of the first millennium. In monarchical terms, such dynasties usually take their name from its founding king, but when you consider that the first King of the Franks was Pepin the Short, you can see why the family preferred the name of his father, Charles Martel. Known as 'The Hammer', though he never took the title of king, Charles was a great warrior who united the Franks and fought off the Muslim invaders from the south, paving the way for Pepin to take the kingship. Though a good king himself, Pepin was succeeded by his son, another Charles, better known in history as Charlemagne, or Charles the Great.

Martel and Charlemagne were both called Carolus in Latin, so the dynasty came to be called Carolingian, though by rights it should have been named after the true founder, and termed 'Peninian'. And that's the long and the short of it.

CHAUVINIST

How does an excessively misogynist person carry the name of Nicolas Chauvin, a simple French soldier in the Napoleonic wars who may or may not have existed? 'Chauvinist', both as a noun and adjective, and the condition of chauvinism, are nowadays almost exclusively used in the context of gender differentiation – male chauvinist pigs, usually.

Yet chauvinist originally meant excessively patriotic, and takes its root from Nicolas Chauvin, who was supposedly a foot soldier in the Army of Napoleon Bonaparte and who was distinguished by his blind patriotism, belief in French superiority and devotion to 'l'Empereur'. He was allegedly badly wounded, even maimed, and may also have been honoured by Bonaparte himself.

The trouble with this eponym is that Chauvin may have been a fantasy as no one has ever found an official army or government record of such a person. His supposed character was used by many writers, however, usually as a figure of fun in the post-Bonaparte era.

In time, Chauvin's excess of love for his country came to be analogously applied to over-the-top zealotry and claims of superiority of any kind. So next time someone calls you a chauvinist, male or female, do not return the insult but content yourself with the realisation that your knowledge, at least, is superior because you now know they are calling you after a man who probably didn't exist.

CHEKHOVIAN; CHEKHOV'S GUN

Anton Chekhov's very Russian convolutions have graced the stage since the plays were written, mostly in the 1890s, following his period as a short-story writer. 'Chekhovian' describes work that resembles that of Chekhov (1860–1904), perhaps set in that period, with ensemble playing and usually full of Russian gloom.

'Chekhov's Gun' is also something invented by the writer. To paraphrase him, 'If you show the audience a gun in the first Act, it must be fired in Act Three.' It's now accepted as a staple of theatre, even if Chekhov doesn't always get the credit.

DAVIDIC

Pertaining to King David of the Israelites, who was a controversial figure even in his own lifetime. He famously slew Goliath of Gath with a slingshot – actually, the stone only knocked out the giant and David hurriedly lopped off his head – giving us the eponymous 'David and Goliath' contest which is used by too many clichéd commentators. David took Uriah the Hittite's wife – beautiful Bathsheba – after sending him to die in battle, and saw his own son, Absalom, killed in a rebellion against his rule.

Yet he established Jerusalem as capital of Israel and God made the Davidic Covenant with him – the promise that the Messiah would come from the line of David, and his kingdom would last for ever. The Davidic psalms, some of which he composed (but not all as was traditionally thought), remain some of the finest prayer-hymns in any religion.

DICKENSIAN

The dickens of the thing about Charles Dickens is that his varied canon should be impossible to encapsulate in a single word.

Think of Charles Dickens' books and most literate people will conjure up a plethora of scenes: Scrooge reaching out to Tiny Tim; Sidney Carton going bravely to the guillotine; Wilkins Micawber saying something will turn up; Oliver Twist asking for more; and Pip loving Estella after the looming presence of Magwitch.

With all the vast array of characters and locations in his books, why does the word 'Dickensian' conjure up an image of London's reeking underbelly in Victorian times?

Some writers have used the adjective to describe Christmas scenes, and others use Dickensian in an almost pejorative sense, as in Dickensian whimsy or sentimentality. By far the most common usage of Dickensian, however, is linked to descriptions of 19th-century London, tales of tenemented slums and fog-bound streets full of orphaned children, heart-of-gold prostitutes and nasty thieves.

Dickensian poverty was very real, and Dickens himself experienced it. His father, John, was a Navy clerk until his rash spending landed him and his family – except young Charles – in Marshalsea Prison until his debts were repaid when an aunt died and left John Dickens a legacy.

The family left prison but continued to struggle, their income boosted partially by Charles working ten hours a day in a shoe-polish factory where working conditions were inhumane.

The genius of the author was to remember these bitter times and write so eloquently about them when he turned to journalism and fiction. He was a superb journalist who wrote shorthand fluently, allowing him to cover events and politics in a swift and memorable manner. It was when he moved into fiction that he truly exposed the horrors in which the poor and downtrodden lived in a style that was both readable and influential – such was the public outrage he occasioned by his books that entire slum areas were cleared and rebuilt.

Charles John Huffam Dickens was born in 1812 and died of a stroke at the age of 58 in 1870, by which time he was the most famous novelist in the world. His critics may say he was overly sentimental and that his characters bordered on caricatures, but his storylines and marvellous prose have survived a century-and-a-half as classics, and his books have never been out of print since they were first produced, mainly as serials in monthly magazines.

Not only did he give us an eponym based on his own

name, but Dickens created many others – we still call unctuous people Uriah Heeps, while Gradgrindian and other eponyms brought about by Dickens have their place in dictionaries.

Yet had he not had a change of heart, we would never have heard of 'Dickensian'. The author started, and meant to continue, his fiction-writing life as 'Boz' – the mispronounced nickname 'Moses' by his younger brother Augustine – as he was already producing major pieces of serious journalism under his own name, and did not want his first, often funny, stories to detract from that work. He was soon persuaded to change to his own name, however, and brought many topics from his London-based journalism into his fiction. He wrote about what he had personally seen and known, creating the Dickensian world that entrances readers to this day.

There is no official statue of Dickens in Britain. In his Will, the author stated that no such public memorial should be erected. Instead, he left us a host of great novels, and characters whose names have become eponyms, while his own eponymous world will live for as long as books are read. What finer memorial could there be?

DRACONIAN

We look back to the Athens of between 2,300 and 2,700 years ago as the breeding ground in which so many of our decent, modern concepts – democracy, drama, philosophy – were wrought. The city was at the heart of Greek cultural development, which in turn influenced so many contemporary and later cultures, including those of Egypt and, above all, Rome. Socrates, Plato and Aristotle alone would have guaranteed Athens its place in history, but add the magnificence of the Acropolis inspired by the genius of Pericles, both a great general and art lover, and so many more writers, artists and philosophers, and you understand why classical Athens was and is so influential.

Yet it was not all sweetness and light in Athens. The city was ruled by powerful families with a system of blood feuds and unwritten laws until a much-maligned yet inspirational figure emerged towards the end of the 7th century BC.

Dracon, or Draco of Athens, basically invented zero tolerance to deal with lawlessness in the city. We know very little about the man himself, but he was clearly in a position of power around 620BC when he wrote the first constitution of Athens.

The laws he laid down were extremely tough, so much so that they were reputed to be written in blood. Death was the punishment for just about every misdemeanour, even that of getting into excessive debt. On the other hand, Dracon was the first lawmaker to differentiate between murder and involuntary killing, a fairer law which underpins the western approach to capital crime to this day.

There is no doubt that, in a few short years, Dracon's laws transformed Athens into a peaceable place, and we can certainly speculate whether the arts and philosophy would have flourished there without his brutal code. His successor Solon came along and brought in a much less cruel legal system, but Dracon had made it possible for him to do so.

The people of Athens allegedly showed their gratitude to Dracon in a bizarre fashion – in the custom of the time, one night in the theatre they honoured him by showering cloaks, capes, hats and other clothing upon him, which promptly buried poor Dracon and smothered him to death.

His name lives on as a byword for harshness, however, and, when JK Rowling was looking for a name for the 'baddie' in her *Harry Potter* series, she conjured up 'Draco' Malfoy.

DYLANESQUE

Bob Dylan, nonpareil wordsmith, was born Robert Allen Zimmerman in Duluth, Minnesota, on 24 May 1941. His remarkable life is just too complex to detail here; suffice to say he is probably the single most influential figure on modern popular music who is alive today.

Dylan's extraordinary achievements as a musician are based largely on the sheer poetry of his lyrics, and his love of word play, figurative allusions and constant creation of verbal imagery have been much copied and sometimes parodied down the decades.

The word 'Dylanesque' describes songs and poems in which the use of words has been inspired by the master himself. Bryan Ferry, former lead singer of Roxy Music, ensured the word had permanence in plastic when he titled his 2007 album of Dylan covers *Dylanesque*. It's well worth a listen, but to really appreciate what is Dylanesque, you have to read and hear some of Bob Dylan's many classic lyrics.

DYONISIAN

Describes an excess of pleasure, usually used in association with drinking sessions and orgies. It derives from the Greek

God Dyonisus, who must have had a whale of a time as he is the god of ecstasy, drinking, winemaking and general madness. His Roman equivalent is Bacchus, from whom we get the word 'Bacchanalian'. It should be noted that, before it became a byword for drunken excess, Bacchanalia was the Latin term for a specific religious festival imported to the city of Rome before 200BC and which, at first, involved only women. Men eventually became involved, however, and by the year 186BC the festivals had become an excuse for mass licentiousness and the Senate banned them.

EDWARDIAN

For a man whose mother's longevity meant he only had a short reign as King of Great Britain and Emperor of India, Edward VII certainly made an impact on the culture – and women – of several nations.

He personally did much to secure the *Entente Cordiale* between Britain and France, and cemented relations between the two powers in his own charming way.

The 'Edwardian era' conjures up visions of style and fun in the years before the Great War, and King Edward's personal approach to life was entirely typical of the age to which he gave his name.

ELIZABETHAN

This eponym usually relates to the reign of Queen Elizabeth I, the 16th-century Virgin Queen who reigned from 1558 to 1603. It was a vital time in British history, coming just after the Reformation and ending in the union of the crowns when James VI of Scotland succeeded the childless Queen. Elizabeth consolidated the Protestant faith in England, saw off the Spanish Armada and rebellious nobles, encouraged theatre and global exploration, and generally ran England in a firm style which saw the country prosper greatly. In many people's opinion, 'Elizabethan' and 'Golden' are interchangeable.

It is yet to be truly appreciated that our own dear Queen Elizabeth has made these last 60 years a second Elizabethan age. She has become a symbol of Christian dutifulness at a time when that concept has been constantly eroded. She has also shown all the Elizabethan qualities – loyalty, courage and vast political nous – to remain the unimpeachable head of state at a time when the world has been utterly transformed.

Perhaps, in time, historians will look back and christen this era, too, as Elizabethan.

FABIAN

Quintus Fabius Maximus Verrucosus, the delaying general, has given his name to a military strategy using attritional tactics, as well as a philosophical approach which could best be described as 'softly, softly, catchee monkey'.

A member of a prominent Roman family, when the Carthaginians under Hannibal attacked down through Italy in the Second Punic War, Fabius made it his *raison de guerre* that it was better to retreat slowly and deny the enemy resources rather than risk everything in a single battle.

When the Roman Army was defeated at Lake Trasimene in June 217BC, Fabius was made 'dictator' which, in ancient Rome, was an honourable office that gave one man power to run the city during a crisis.

He refused to confront Hannibal, and his Fabian strategy was not popular, so that the dictator was given the nickname '*cunctator*' which is the Latin for 'delayer'. But by law, Fabius could not remain dictator permanently and the following year new generals led the Roman Army to an even greater defeat at Cannae in August 216BC. Fabius duly came back into power and this time the Romans listened to him, so that Hannibal was frustrated at every turn, but never in all-out battle, as he tried to take over the whole Italian peninsula. It took ten years, but the Carthaginians eventually went home.

Fabius was acclaimed as the 'Shield of Rome' by the time of his death at the age of 76 or 77 in 203BC, and the following year Scipio led the Romans over to Carthage in North Africa and defeated them at the Battle of Zama, ending the war decisively in Rome's favour.

Fabius also lends his name to the Fabian Society, the British organisation which promotes the advance of democratic socialism through gradual reform. That an Italian 'dictator' gave his name to a modern, left-wing movement in Britain shows you how wide-ranging eponyms can be.

FAUSTIAN

In German legend, the alchemist and scholar Faust made a deal with the devil in which he accepted eternal damnation after death in return for a life of pleasure based on magical powers. We still call this deal a 'Faustian pact', the story of Faust having remained pretty much constant through more than five centuries of adaptation, starting with Christopher Marlowe's play *The Tragical History of the Life and Death of Doctor Faustus* (1604), Goethe's drama *Faust*, several operas, many prose and poetry works, the musical *Damn Yankees* (1955) and numerous films.

It's a powerful story, almost mythical, but it may well have been based on a real man – Johann Georg Faust who lived from around 1480 to 1540, and was an astrologer and alchemist. Since he wrote horoscopes and generally performed magic tricks around southern Germany in a God-fearing age, he gained a reputation as a man with a dark side. Indeed, he was accused of everything from fraud to sodomy by his enemies, who included the all-powerful Catholic Church. The fact that he supposedly joined the Protestant cause as soon as it sprang up may well have occasioned the Church's disdain, and he was condemned as being in league with the devil. This Dr Faustus also died in an explosion allegedly caused by his own experiments, thus getting the legend off to a suitably gruesome start.

FREUDIAN SLIP

Admit it – you don't know what a parapraxis is. Call it a Freudian slip, however, and everyone knows what you are talking about. A slip of the tongue or pen caused by an unconscious thought takes its name from Sigmund Freud (1856–1939), the Austrian whose psychoanalysis theories defined our minds.

GARGANTUAN

Gargantua was the gigantic creation of François Rabelais (see *Rabelaisian* below) in his series of books called *Gargantua* and *Pantagruel*. The former was father of the latter and both were giants, but it is 'gargantuan' we use – 'pantagruellan' being somewhat clumsy.

GEORGIAN

When used in historical or architectural terms, this word refers to the period of King George and items produced at that time, and not the country of Georgia or the State of the USA. It is possibly a unique eponym in that it derives from not one man's name, but four. Kings George I, II, III and IV ruled Britain from 1714 to 1830, and the first 90-odd years were very much influenced by their Hanoverian antecedents. The Georges liked order and control, as shown by their abhorrence of social reform at home and the French and American Revolutions. Yet they also encouraged the arts and their chief achievement was the consolidation of the United Kingdom once the Jacobites (see below) had been defeated, with the start of the British Empire's expansion also taking place during their reigns. The Regency period ran from 1811 to 20, when the later King George IV was briefly let off the leash, while his father, George III, after being mentally incapacitated, ended the Georgian era, leaving visible signs of its existence in various cities such as Bath and Edinburgh's New Town.

GILBERTIAN

Though Sir Tim Rice might disagree, William Schwenck Gilbert (1836–1911) is without doubt the greatest librettist in the history of British musical theatre. His comic operas with Sir Arthur Sullivan delighted audiences with their cleverness that relied on Gilbert's lyrical trickery. Such sparkling wit relying on word play has often been called

'Gilbertian' in the past, but now the word is often used to mean whimsical, which Gilbert rarely was – in his heyday he was renowned, perhaps unfairly, for being abrasive as a person and cutting in his lyrics.

GRADGRINDIAN

The obsessive, soulless Mr Thomas Gradgrind is the schoolmaster and later MP in Charles Dickens' *Hard Times* who bellows 'fact, fact, fact' at his pupils and is generally inflexible and dictatorial even to his own children. His name has become a byword for sheer toil and a miserable emotionless existence, even though, in *Hard Times*, Gradgrind himself comes to realise his philosophy is flawed when his daughter Louisa breaks down and repudiates his Gradgrindian approach.

GREGORIAN

This adjective is normally applied to two things – Gregorian chant and the Gregorian calendar. Pope Gregory I (c.540–604AD), known as Saint Gregory the Great, is said to have encouraged the former around the year 600AD as a variety of plainsong or plainchant, the oldest form of vocal music in the Christian Church. Gregory XIII (1502–85) commissioned the revision of the old Julian calendar (see below) and gave his name to the calendar which is now the accepted version worldwide. In order to accommodate the new calendar, 11 days were 'missed'. The Reformation saw a number of countries refuse to accept the papal decree about the new calendar, so that a dual date system was introduced in a lot of places.

HERCULEAN

The Greek mythological figure Heracles (Latin version Hercules) almost had it all. Semi-divine, stronger and more athletic than any man alive, but perhaps not the brightest spark in the Olympian pantheon. According to the ancient myths, he annoyed the Goddess Hera simply by being the son of a beautiful mortal and her husband Zeus, and she eventually drove Heracles mad, so that he killed his own children. To earn redemption, he was forced to undertake his famous 12 labours, including the cleaning of the Augean stables – they had 1,000 horses and had not been cleaned for 30 years – which he accomplished by diverting a couple of rivers through them. Heracles had many other adventures, including seeking the Gold Fleece with Jason and the Argonauts, and generally went about fighting and killing and having women trouble, not least with Hera, because he was definitely more passionate than intellectual. It is because of his 12 labours that we speak of someone facing a Herculean task.

HOMERIC

Pertaining to the epics of Homer, the most famous of the ancient Greek writers. Homer's *Iliad* and *Odyssey* arguably started literature, but we know very little about the author himself. We are not even sure he was blind, as was reported in ancient times. His epic poems, however, have lasted through nearly three millennia, and that is almost Homeric in itself.

JOYCEAN

James Joyce (1882–1941) was an Irish writer who continues to puzzle students of English literature 70 years after his death. His style was revolutionary in its day, and, while many have tried to copy Joycean writing, particularly the stream of consciousness style he devised, none has equalled the man himself.

JUNGIAN

Carl Gustav Jung (1876–1961) was a Swiss psychiatrist who pioneered analytical psychology and developed several important concepts such as the collective unconscious and synchronicity, as well as laying out what makes a person introvert or extrovert. His interest in psychology and mental illness may have been inspired by his mother who was a depressive and complained of being visited by unearthly spirits at night. Spooky.

JUVENALIAN

Juvenal (c.65–135AD) didn't invent sarcasm, he perfected it. In a series of brilliant writings, he dissected Roman society with wit, personal invective and no little anger. Juvenalian satire has a long tradition in literature, and, though many modern comedians are strictly juvenile, a few do reach juvenalian heights.

KAFKAESQUE

Franz Kafka (1883–1924) was a Prague-born writer who viewed reality as an experience of surreality mixed with menace, and his literary output mixes the absurd and malevolent in an entertaining yet uncomfortable fashion. His background as an insurance assessor gave him plenty of access to the courts and legal systems he savaged in his books, especially *The Trial*.

Our own age has seen Kafka's fears writ large. There are times when only the word 'kafkaesque' can be used to describe the sinister and bizarre activities of bureaucracies everywhere.

KEYNESIAN

As arguably the single most influential economist of the 20th century, Englishman John Maynard Keynes (1883–1946) helped to define the modern age. His concepts on monetary policy and fiscal stimulus won support from politicians and the public alike and he is one of the few economists whose name is generally recognised by those with little interest in economic matters.

LUCULLAN

Roman general and consul Lucius Licinius Lucullus loved a banquet. He gave the very biggest and best in Rome in the first century BC, and his name became associated with everything from orgies to gluttonous feasts, which apparently is what his banquets turned into.

MACABRE

Nowadays we use this word to describe bizarre and strange things in general, but its original meaning in French was specifically to do with death and the gruesomeness of dying. The *danse macabre* was the Dance of Death, a frequent subject in the art and literature of the 14th and 15th centuries, in which the figure of Death was depicted leading the final dance of poor and rich alike. Given the outbreaks of plague and famine at that time, the Dance of Death was something people anticipated happening to them pretty soon.

Some scholars suggest 'macabre' came from the Maccabees, the ancient Jewish family led by Judas Maccabeus whose history and doctrines feature in the Bible, though not in the version of the Bible used by most Protestant denominations.

The Second Book of the Maccabees is heavily concerned with death and dying, and includes prayers for the dead as well as the story of the Maccabean martyrs – seven brothers who were executed along with their mother and teacher – which was a very popular tradition in the Christian Church until the Middle Ages when the word 'macabre' first appeared.

Interestingly, the Roman Catholic Church still lists the Holy Maccabees as saints and martyrs, even though they all lived and died decades before Jesus Christ was born. That is not macabre, but certainly bizarre.

MACHIAVELLIAN

Let there be no mistake, 'machiavellian' is one eponym which entirely fits the person whose name it bears.

Apologists have often tried to make out that Niccolo di Bernardi dei Machiavelli (1469–1527) was not as bad as he is painted, but you only have to read *The Prince* to see what a thoroughgoing advocate of chicanery he really was.

His political philosophy advocated rule by a not-so-benign dictator whose dictum should always be 'it is much safer to be feared than loved'. For Machiavelli, expediency was everything, and scruples were to be retained only as far as it assisted the maintenance of a ruler's good image. Cruelty was to be a prince's stock in trade, though pragmatism demanded that the ruler try to avoid losing the respect of his courtiers in particular. He once wrote that 'force and prudence' were the qualities of good government. Genuine compassion? True mercy? They were for weak fools.

Considering him to be a writer and philosopher of note, Machiavelli's supporters say *The Prince* was a satire aimed at upsetting Florence's ruler, Lorenzo di Piero de Medici, grandson of Lorenzo 'Il Magnifico' de Medici. If so, why was the book written in 1513 not published until 1532, five years after Machiavelli's death and thirteen years after Lorenzo died from syphilis?

In his other works, such as *The Discourses* and *The Art of War* – his own favourite book – Machiavelli gave enough hints that he really did advocate a cynical approach to governance. In *The Prince*, he brought his undoubted talents as a playwright, poet and civil servant – he had been secretary of the chancery of the Florentine Republic – to bear on the question posed since the time of Socrates, Plato and Aristotle, namely what was the best form of government for a city State.

The key point to know is that, before he wrote the book, Machiavelli was tortured by the Medici for his support for the Republic against the family. Given his self-acknowledged cunning, it is thus far more likely that he wrote *The Prince* and dedicated it to Lorenzo to get back into the ruler's good books, which appears to have happened as Machiavelli was allowed to retire to his estate and write his books, which included his eight-volume *Florentine Histories* – paid for by the patronage of the Medici family who took his advice on many matters.

To go from rebelliously opposing the Medici to being their employee and counsellor – that was truly machiavellian.

What is also undoubtedly true of Machiavelli is the impact his thought had, both while he lived and ever since. His books were widely read by kings and politicians, and he was reviled and praised by commentators in his own lifetime. By the end of the 16th century, his name had become a byword for trickery – Schmidt's *Shakespeare Lexicon and Quotation Dictionary* notes three usages in the Bard's plays, particularly the line 'Am I a Machiavel?' in *The Merry Wives of Windsor*.

Since then, every dictator from the Emperor Napoleon to Benito Mussolini has admitted to being influenced by Machiavelli.

There is proof in stone of the esteem in which Machiavelli was held, at least in his native Florence, and of the fact that 'machiavellian' had become a famous term in its own right. If you visit the Franciscan Basilica of Santa Croce (Holy Cross) in Florence, you will see that it is the Florentine equivalent of Westminster Abbey in that its monuments honour great people of the city. Not far from the monuments dedicated to Galileo, Michelangelo and locally born Florence Nightingale is the splendid monument to 'Nickolaus Machiavelli', erected in the 18th century. The splendid male figure in marble is not the man himself, but the allegorical figure of Diplomacy, for which he was also remembered.

The monument bears the Latin inscription 'Tanto

Nomini Nullum Par Elogium', which roughly translates as 'no eulogy would be enough for such a name'.

The inscription recognises that the eponym 'machiavellian' had long ago passed into the language. You get the feeling that Machiavelli himself would have liked that.

MAUDLIN

As one of Christ's followers who may or may not have been a prostitute before she joined the Apostles, St Mary Magdelene is one of the more interesting people in the Bible. It was she who first encountered the risen Christ, and possibly for that reason she has always been of fascination to scholars and artists alike. The New Testament records Mary Magdalene cried and was sorry, and so being tearful and contrite came to be Magdelene-like, with the English pronunciation of her name eventually being rendered as it is spelled phonetically.

NAPOLEONIC

He was not as short as has been suggested and, as a figure in French history, Napoleon Bonaparte towers over everyone else. His name is associated with brandy, wars, the entire age. The wee Emperor couldn't beat Wellington (see Chapter 7) and left us his name rather than a boot.

NIETZSCHEAN

Pertaining to the works and philosophy of Friedrich Nietzsche (1844–1900), who was the king of quotable quotes among 19th-century philosophers, his most famous statement being that 'God is dead'. His thoughts on religion – best summed up in his saying 'faith is not wanting to know what is true' – scandalised Europe, while his theories on a 'superman' higher species are said to have influenced Nazism.

ORWELLIAN

His real name was Eric Arthur Blair (1903–50), but, writing as George Orwell, this English former colonial policeman got many things right about the society he was willing to predict in books such *Animal Farm* and especially *1984*. In these days of omnipresent CCTV and text messages that read like Newspeak, too often we are living his Orwellian nightmare.

PALLADIAN

'It's all Greek to me' is something Andrea Palladio (1508–80) probably never said, but the Italian created the style of Greek- and Roman-influenced architecture that bears his name. By going back to ancient Greece and Rome for his inspiration, Palladianism emphasised a formal style that became the most important architectural influence of the 16th–19th centuries. Every building he personally designed is located in Italy, but there are examples of Palladian architecture around the world.

PAVLOVIAN

The Pavlovian response or classic conditioning is one of the most important theories in physiology. It was proven by Ivan Petrovich Pavlov (1849–1936) in a famous experiment in which he showed that dogs could be conditioned to salivate at the unconscious thought of food associated with a ringing bell. Pavlov, who won the Nobel Prize for Physiology in 1904, had trained to be a priest before taking up science with a lifelong wholeheartedness – even on his deathbed he was experimenting on himself as he prepared to die. Another little-known fact about Pavlov is that his wife Sara suffered a miscarriage through having to walk fast everywhere to keep up with her husband.

PLATONIC

Refers to Plato (c.452–347BC) who was the pupil of Socrates in Athens who recorded his master's sayings and wrote about his trial and death. Plato himself became a great philosopher in his own right, and taught Aristotle, the three of them forming the great triumvirate who effectively invented western philosophy. Platonic philosophy very much centred on his theories of realism, while politically he outlined an ideal city ruled by a benevolent philosopher despot in his book *The Republic*.

Platonic relationships are so called because Plato outlined just such a form of love in his work *Symposium*, one of his *Dialogues*. The original meaning of a love inspired by spirituality nowadays sees 'Platonic' meaning sexless.

PROMETHEAN

Its normal sense meaning original and creative, this eponym derives from Prometheus, humanity's first champion in Greek mythology. One of the Titans who fell out with Zeus of Olympus, he was the ultimate clever-clogs, who taught humans everything from medicine to writing. He also stole the secret of fire and gave it to mankind, for which Zeus conjured up a very nasty punishment for him, chaining him to a rock where an eagle ate his liver every day only for it to grow back again at night.

PROTEAN

We use this word to describe versatility. It derives from Greek mythology, from the Old Man of the Sea, otherwise known as the shape-changing god Proteus, the son of Poseidon. 'Proteus Syndrome' is a horrific, disabling disease which leads to multiple deformations in sufferers.

PYTHONESQUE

Bizarre, outlandish, but very, very funny, the Monty Python's Flying Circus team revolutionised humour with their sketch-based, television comedy series. The Ministry of Silly Walks, 'The Lumberjack Song', the Dead Parrot sketch and their search on the big screen for the Holy Grail, as well as the *Life of Brian* – so many memorable skits and movies shot through with their trademark irreverence. Although they last worked together shortly before Graham Chapman died in 1989, the Pythons are still influencing comedy today.

PYRRHIC

Pyrrhus, king of Epirus (319–272BC), won a battle but at great cost. He was a Greek who tried to unite the various Greek States against the increasing power of Rome. He led a Greek Army into Italy and, at the Battle of Asculum in southern Italy in 279BC, he defeated a numerically superior Roman Army but lost many of his own troops. He was congratulated on his triumph and replied 'one more victory like that will finish me'. Practically from then on, such a bloody and costly win became known as a Pyrrhic victory.

Pyrrhus himself met a peculiar end. Invading the city of Argos, an old woman threw down a roof tile which knocked him for six, enabling an opponent to chop off the king's head.

QUIXOTIC

In the first great European comic novel, Miguel de Cervantes Saavedra (1547–1616) created one of the seminal figures in world literature, Don Quixote. He was a middle-aged gentleman gone soft in the head, who was obsessed with chivalry and romance and, being quite deluded, went off on an adventure with his dimwit neighbour Sancho Panza. Quixote tilted at windmills, and turned just about every available encounter into a chivalrous quest carried out in the name of his lady Dulcinea – in reality an unknowing farm girl – before returning home disillusioned. It is that practice of doing something strange, perhaps knowing that it will be ultimately unrewarding, which we describe as 'quixotic'.

RABELAISIAN

It is sometimes incorrectly used to mean out of control or even orgiastic, but the original meaning of the word is to describe something as similar to the works of François Rabelais himself – down-to-earth and humorous.

In his published works, Rabelais (1494–1553) was many things that most writers of the era were not – satirical, funny, humanist and full of coarseness such as double entendres which raise eyebrows even today. His best-known works are the novels *Gargantua* and *Pantagruel*, the former giving us the eponym 'gargantuan' (see above).

Rabelais was a doctor by profession, but his sympathies lay very much with the common people, and that earthiness and humanist sympathies saw him condemned by the Church. He is said to have died muttering that he was 'going to the Great Perhaps'.

RUBENESQUE

The artist Peter Paul Rubens (1577–1640) loved big, voluptuous girls, and painted plenty of them. So many, indeed, that a plump, curvy woman is often described as 'Rubenesque', especially if she's naked in a painting.

RUNYONESQUE

Damon Runyon (1880–1946) wrote about a huge cast of characters in his short stories set in and around Broadway in New York. The big-city low-lifers he depicted ranged from two-bit gangsters to showgirls, and Runyon was clearly writing from personal experience as many of the characters could be identified with real-life people. Runyon was cremated when he died and, according to his instructions, his ashes were scattered from an aircraft down on to Broadway.

SEMITIC

The Semitic peoples of the Middle East are supposedly all descended from Noah's son Shem. It is the Semitic languages and cultures, rather than a shared genetic inheritance, which determined if someone was or is a

Semite. According to the Bible, Shem lived until he was 600, and one of his descendants was Abraham.

SHAVIAN

Since the eponym is derived from his name, we can say with certainty that George Bernard Shaw (1856–1950) was the first, and best, exponent of Shavian wit. The Irish writer, political theorist and co-founder of the London School of Economics made many famous witticisms: 'England and America are two countries separated by a common language'; 'I often quote myself, it adds spice to my conversation'; and 'If all economists were laid end to end, they would not reach a conclusion' are just three.

SOCRATIC

'I know enough to know that I will never know enough' is a rough approximation of the greatest piece of wisdom enunciated by Socrates (469–399BC). His school in ancient Athens became the centre for a new type of philosophical learning, and his most famous pupil, Plato, recorded many of his master's musings.

The man himself was an oddball. Apparently quite ugly, after serving as a soldier, he took to walking round Athens barefoot and stinking as he refused to wash daily. His Socratic method of philosophical inquiry has influenced much of western thought, yet the man himself appears to have been a walking disaster area, upsetting people in power. Ordered by the Athenian authorities to kill himself in punishment for 'corrupting the youth', he calmly drank poisonous hemlock.

STAKHANOVITE

The human robot of the USSR Alexey Stakhanov (1906–77) was plucked from obscurity by the propaganda machine of the Soviet Union to become the poster boy of the Government's drive to increase productivity in coal mines and elsewhere. Stakhanov broke all sorts of records with his ability to hew coal quicker than anyone else, and his achievements were lauded to inspire Soviet workers to emulate him.

There have been doubts about whether he did actually cut 227 tonnes of coal in a single shift, but what is not in doubt is that his name is now attached to colossal feats in the workplace, and workers who triumph with their drudgery.

STENTORIAN

In the world's first great surviving historical-mythical novel, Homer's *Iliad*, we find a description of Stentor (book V, v 783), reportedly a herald who had a voice as loud as 50 men. Unfortunately, Stentor took on the herald of the Olympian gods, Hermes, in a shouting match and lost – fatally so, as his shouting proved too much for his all-too-human lungs.

He remains the precursor of town criers everywhere, as well as loud politicians such as the Reverend Ian Paisley and actors such as Brian Blessed and Gerard 'this is Sparta' Butler.

Stentorian nowadays sometimes means 'over the top' as much as loud. That is an obvious development of the word.

Stentor also gave his name to a genus of single-cell organisms found on algae. These protozoa look like trumpets, hence the name of Stentor, though you would need a microscope to check the resemblance, as Stentors are only a few millimetres long.

STONEWALL, STONEWALLER

For some inexplicable reason, the nickname of an American Civil War general is now routinely used to describe a penalty in British football, as in 'it's a stonewaller, ref'. The original Stonewall was Confederate General Thomas Jonathan Jackson (1824–63) who gained his nickname in the First Battle of Bull Run in 1861, when a fellow general is reputed to have said 'there's Jackson standing like a stone wall'. Jackson's troops refused to yield and suffered heavy losses, becoming known thereafter as the Stonewall brigade while he became 'Stonewall Jackson'. He did not enjoy the name for too long, as he died of pneumonia two years later after being accidentally shot by his own side.

Any form of firm defence in sport or other activity soon became known as stonewall, but stonewaller is a recent development, coming from the seemingly endless ability of footballers and commentators to mangle the English language – somebody clearly thought 'stonewall' meant certain, and then '-er' was added to change the eponym's meaning entirely. But that's the trouble with followers of the beautiful game – their brains are in their feet.

STYGIAN

Usually only seen describing darkness or depth, this word comes from the River Styx, one of the nine rivers of the Underworld in Greek mythology. But Styx was also the name of a goddess, the chief supporter of Zeus in the war of the Titans, and therefore a 'goodie'. Perhaps the ancient Greeks got confused.

TAWDRY

How can a word that means trashy, vulgar and shabby be derived from a saintly virgin?

Saint Etheldreda, or Aethelhtryth, was one of the most famous saints of early Christian England. Her life story was written in ancient books and sculptures and, as with all such saints, some liberties were taken with her tale, not least by the Venerable Bede, chronicler supreme and legendarist of Ye Olde Englande.

A 7th-century Saxon princess, Saint Etheldreda's father Anna (sic) was king of what is now East Anglia, and was supposedly descended from Odin, the chief Norse god. Like her father and three sisters who also all became saints, Etheldreda was an enthusiastic convert to Christianity. She wanted to become a nun, however, and vowed to remain celibate.

This proved a trifle problematic. For dynastic reasons, her father married her off to two royal princes in succession, the first a Prince Tonbert, who never demanded his conjugal rights.

The second, Prince Egfrith, was just a boy when they married, but grew up to be a lusty man and also the King of Bernicia, or Northumbria as we know it.

Egfrith eventually begged his father-in-law to order that Etheldreda be 'fully' a wife to him, but she resisted and ran away. Miraculously prevented from following her – the sea off East Anglia rose up between them and the tide stayed high for seven hours, or so it is alleged – Egfrith concluded that God was on her side and allowed Etheldreda to enter a convent.

Having acquired the Isle of Ely as a dowry for her first marriage, Etheldreda founded a monastery there for both monks and nuns and became its first Abbess. She was renowned for her piety and took cold baths to mortify her flesh, though she did allow herself four warm baths a year at Festival times – but only if the other nuns had used the water first.

Etheldreda died of a throat tumour in 679, a fate which in typical fashion she blamed as a sort of Christian karma on her past as a royal princess who had once loved good clothes and fine necklaces. An operation to remove the tumour failed, and left a gaping wound on her dead throat.

According to Bede, when her coffin was opened 17 years after her death, her face had been restored to youthful bloom and the wound had healed. Not surprisingly, with such a story doing the rounds, a cult grew up around the Abbess who by popular acclaim became not only a saint but also patroness of those with throat problems. The male patron saint of throats was St Blaise, whose feast day is 3 February – the author well recalls as a child taking part in the ceremony of the Blessing of the Throats when two candles lashed into the form of a cross were placed around his throat and the blessing intoned.

The most famous Blessing of the Throats ceremony in the UK takes place each year on St Blaise's Day at St Etheldreda's Church in Ely Place in London, which has survived reformations, civil war and being bombed by the Nazis to be the second-oldest Catholic church in England.

It seems almost pitiful that this remarkable woman is remembered by such a word as 'tawdry', but that's the English language for you; during the transition from Anglo-Saxon to modern English, the name Etheldreda somehow became Audrey, as it remains to this day.

As a mark of respect to the story of Etheldreda/Audrey and her throat, and seeking her Heavenly protection, pilgrims to Ely were the first to wear St Audrey's Laces, scarf-like lace neckties which were worn around the time of the annual St Audrey's Fair on 17 October. Typical English elision soon made them 't'awdry laces'.

In time, as with most souvenirs, these laces became somewhat adulterated, cheap and nasty. When the Puritans came along – they were particularly strong around the Isle of Ely where Oliver Cromwell made his home – they banned all such dressiness and poured disdain on 'tawdry laces', so that 'tawdry' became a description for things that are tacky and tasteless, which the holy and virginal St Etheldreda never was.

TERPSICHOREAN

Relating to dance, this adjective comes from the muse Terpsichore in ancient Greek mythology. Her name means 'delighting in dance', and not only did she like a jig, she was the muse of choruses in drama, too.

THESPIAN

Call an actor a 'luvvie', and they will nearly always say, 'No, I'm a thespian.'

Thespis was an actor who lived in 6th-century Greece. He

was the first actor to play a character in a play on stage, a new style of drama that was called tragedy. He was also the first documented luvvie – sorry, thespian – to win an award for acting. It is not known whether he cried during his acceptance speech.

TITCHY

This can be an unpleasant word as it is usually used to describe somebody of a small stature, but the original 'titch' was not small at all. The Titchborne Claimant, Arthur Orton (1834–98), submitted a legal claim to be recognised as Sir Roger Titchborne, the heir to one of England's richest fortunes. He lost, was exposed as an impostor, and served ten years in prison for his crime. Orton was not minuscule – indeed, he was obese – but, for a joke, Harry Relph (1867–1928), a famous English music hall comedian who was just 4ft 6in or 1.37m tall, took his stage name, Little Tich, from the Claimant, and the great British public made the word stick.

VICTORIAN

Pertaining to the reign of Queen Victoria (1819–1901) who inherited the throne from her grandfather, George IV, at the age of 18, starting the Victorian era which lasted until her death. We hear much these days about Victorian values, as Her Majesty was the embodiment of civilised behaviour. Sadly, today's public figures seem to find it harder and harder to live up to the standards set by the UK's longest-serving monarch.

VITRUVIAN

The eponymous Man is arguably the world's most famous

drawing. Leonardo da Vinci's 1487 creation was inspired by Roman sage and architect Marcus Vitruvius Pollio who wrote *On Architecture* in the 1st century BC. Sadly, we know little about him, except that he was a multi-talented builder and engineer and served in the Army of Julius Caesar.

WAGNERIAN
Though it is hard to define exactly, most people know what they mean when mentioning Wagnerian music – loud and proud, as in the overblown operas of the German composer and conductor Wilhelm Richard Wagner (1813–83).

WILDEAN
Relating to Irish playwright Oscar Fingal O'Flahertie Wills Wilde (1854–1900) and his wit and wisdom, rather than the tragedy of his imprisonment for homosexuality.

· 2 ·

SITE AND SOUND

There are literally thousands of places named after people –
too many to recount them all, in fact. This chapter therefore
deals with only major geographical features, countries, cities
and towns.

There are also eponyms derived from the names of places,
but only the best known of these will feature.

EPONYMOUS GEOGRAPHICAL FEATURES

AMUNDSEN SEA
Roald Amundsen (1872–1928) was a Norwegian explorer
who was the first person to reach the South Pole in 1911.
Several places in Antarctica are named after him, as is this sea
off Antarctica.

ANNAPURNA
The Annapurna range of peaks in the Himalayas and the
mountain itself are named after the Hindu goddess of

nourishment. The mountain, Annapurna I, rises to 8,091m (26,545ft), and has the highest fatality ratio of any mountain above 8,000m with approximately four in ten climbers failing to return from summit ascents.

BAFFIN ISLAND AND BAY

Baffin Island is the fifth-largest island in the world, and the largest in Canada. The adjacent eponymous bay is really a sea, and part of the North Atlantic ocean, with the Davis Strait (named after English explorer John Davis 1550–1605) connecting it to the Labrador Sea. The Baffin in question was William Baffin (1584–1622), a lowly born explorer and navigator who gained fame for his remarkably accurate charting and measuring of Arctic regions, for his discovery of the seas and land areas north and west of Greenland that bear his name and those of his patrons, and for his experiments in longitude. Maybe he can be forgiven for never actually discovering the Northwest Passage after years of trying.

BARENTS SEA

The sea north of Norway and Russia is named after Dutch explorer Willem Barentsz (c.1550–97) who explored and mapped the area. Barentsz and his crew on his third voyage north were trapped on the ice-bound island Novaya Zemlya for the winter, but most survived in a wooden lodge they built until they tried to sail south in June. While Barentsz died aboard while studying his charts. The lodge survived intact until it was discovered almost three centuries later.

BERING SEA

This massive area of water is the fourth-largest sea in the world and the largest named after a person. The sea lies to the east of Siberia and the west of Alaska and is named after Vitus Bering (1681–1741), a Danish navigator who joined the Russian Navy in the service of Tsar Peter the Great (1682–1725). Bering charted the whole area to the north of the Pacific and sailed through the Straits named after him but, on his last voyage at the age of 60, he took ill and died on an island near Kamchatka, which was later named after him.

BRAHMAPUTRA RIVER

This name means 'son of Brahma' who was the Hindu god of creation. The river is one of the most important in Asia, flowing 2,900km (1,800 miles) from the Himalayas via the Ganges delta to the Bay of Bengal. The lower part of the river is sacred to Hindus.

DOLOMITES

The Italian mountain range used to be known as the pale or white mountains but, in the late 18th century, the French soldier and geologist Déodat Gratet de Dolomieu (1750–1801) was on a field trip when he found a rock that was typical of the area. He described it in a journal and, as a result, the type of rock was called 'dolomite' after him, with the mountains gradually taking on that name after Dolomieu became rather famous. He had been an adventurous type since adolescence, killing a colleague in the Knights of Malta order in a duel at the age of 18. He survived the French Revolution, but only just, and threw in his lot with Napoleon. By ill luck, he was imprisoned in Sicily for nearly two years during France's war with the Kingdom of the Two Sicilies and that affected his health. Regardless of whether their countries were fighting Napoleon or not, scientists across Europe called for his release, which was eventually gained when Napoleon invaded Italy, the Emperor demanding his freedom as part of the peace treaty. Dolomieu did not survive long after his release but, by the middle of the 19th century, his name was inextricably attached to the mountains.

DOYLE'S DELIGHT

The highest peak in Belize, rising to 1124m (3675ft), is in the Cockscomb range in the southern part of the country, the former British Honduras. It was only recognised as the highest point in the country in recent decades, with Victoria Peak – that ubiquitous monarch – being considered higher prior to someone checking. Named only in 1989 by Sharon Matola (b. 1954), the American founder of Belize Zoo, Doyle's Delight is named after Sir Arthur Ignatius Conan Doyle (1859–1930), the Edinburgh-born creator of Sherlock Holmes who also wrote the adventures of Professor Challenger, central figure of his novel *The Lost World*, which features dinosaurs being found on a South American plateau, the sort of place Doyle delighted in describing, even if he never visited it.

GULF OF ST LAWRENCE

The world's largest estuary, like the river which flows into it, bears the name of St Lawrence (c.225–258), one of seven deacons martyred in Rome by the Emperor Valerian. Having been cooked to death on a griddle, Lawrence is patron saint of chefs, as well as librarians and comedians. The Gulf and river received their name thanks to Jacques Cartier (1491–1557), the French explorer who first sailed into the river on St Lawrence's feast day, 10 August, in 1535.

HUDSON BAY

The world's second-largest bay and, in reality, a shallow sea connected to the Atlantic Ocean by the Hudson Strait. The Hudson name is poignant, as it honours Henry Hudson who explored and mapped the bay in 1610 in a ship called *Discovery*.

Hudson, who had earlier mapped the river at New York which bears his name, was set adrift on the waters of the bay in a small open boat with his son and loyal crewmen after a mutiny. Not surprisingly, Hudson and his companions were never seen again and they are presumed to have died in the bay.

HUMBOLDT CURRENT

One of the most important ocean systems on the planet, the Humboldt Current is a massive, cooling current of water in the Pacific Ocean that flows north along the west coast of South America. A fifth of the world's catch of fish is to be found in its waters. It is named after Baron Friedrich Heinrich Alexander van Humboldt (1769–1859), a German naturalist born in Berlin whose five-year voyage and discoveries in Central and South America make him one of the great figures of geographical science.

ISMOIL SOMONI PEAK

Formerly Stalin Peak and Communism Peak, the highest mountain in the former Soviet Union territories is now called after Ismoil Somoni or Ismail Samani (d. 907), leader of the Samani dynasty which conquered the region now known as the country of Tajikistan in which the mountain rises to a height of 7,495m (24,590ft). Somoni is also the name of Tajikistan's currency, and Ismoil is still revered by the nation as a devout and just Muslim ruler.

MACGILLICUDDY'S REEKS

What links American singer and songwriter the late Warren Zevon to an ancient Irish clan, a sect of the even more ancient O'Sullivans?

The answer is Macgillicuddy's Reeks, a range of mountains in County Kerry in the south-west of Ireland. Also known as the Black Stacks (Na Cruacha Dubha), the range contains the tallest mountain in Ireland, Carrantuohill, which is 1,039m high.

According to the *Encyclopaedia Britannica*, the range's geological basis 'is a long anticlinal range of Devonian sandstones that was strongly glaciated, producing many valleys, serrated ridges, and peaks'. In other words, not an easy walk, especially on one of Ireland's 'Vivaldi' days – four seasons of weather in a few hours.

By that old process of transference, the Black Stacks got their English name from clan Macgillicuddy who owned much of the range in the 18th century, and whose name gradually became attached to the mountains, local people describing them as 'Macgillicuddy's hay ricks', hence reeks.

Warren Zevon, best known for his hit song 'Werewolves of London', co-wrote the song 'Macgillicuddy's Reeks' with Northern Irish poet Paul Muldoon. It appeared on the album *My Ride's Here* released shortly before Zevon's death from cancer in 2003. It's a lively song and should be better known, a bit like the Reeks themselves.

MACKENZIE RIVER

With the Peace and Finlay rivers, this is the longest river system in Canada, second-longest in North America and thirteenth-longest in the world at 2,635 miles (4,241km). It is the longest river in the world named after an individual. Formerly known as the Dehco and Disappointment River, in 1789 a Scotsman called Alexander Mackenzie (1764–1820) travelled down its length hoping to find the Pacific Ocean. Instead, he found that the river emptied into the Arctic Ocean, hence Disappointment.

Mackenzie later made the first crossing of northern North America. He was knighted and the Disappointment River was renamed in his honour. He also has a rose named after him – that fact is not so well known.

MAGELLANIC STRAIT; THE STRAITS OF MAGELLAN

The name of the first man to sail round the world was not Ferdinand Magellan (1480–1521), although he was first commander of the Spanish expedition which achieved the feat from 1519 to 1522. The Portuguese Magellan was, however, the first European to navigate this dangerous strait between South America's mainland and the island of Tierra del Fuego in 1520. Sadly for Magellan, his journey came to an abrupt halt in the Philippines the following year when he was killed at the Battle of Mactan in quite horrible fashion, hacked to death by angry natives. Spanish navigator Juan Sebastiáno Elcano (1486–1526) took command and completed the voyage, but his name is barely remembered.

MOUNT EVEREST

Mount Chomolungma or Sagarmatha – sorry, it just doesn't sound right to western ears. These are the names of the world's highest mountain in the Tibetan and Nepalese languages, the former being the name used in China which now controls Tibet.

In 1856, after years of effort by the British, Andrew Waugh (1810–78), the Surveyor General of India, fixed the height of what was known as Peak XV at 8,840m (29,002ft).

Waugh proposed that the mountain be named Everest in honour of his predecessor in office. This was accepted, despite Sir George Everest (1790–1866) himself objecting as he had always tried to use native names, or as near as he could render them in English.

Technically, Everest is only the highest point on Earth, as the mountain Mauna Kea in Hawaii measures more than 10,200m or 32,000ft from summit to its base on the ocean floor.

Chomolungma is also possibly an eponym since it translates as Goddess Mother of the World.

MOUNT GODWIN AUSTEN

This is the former name, still used by some people, of the world's second-highest mountain, now more prosaically known as K2. Shared between China and Pakistan, the K stands for Karakoram, the range of which it is a member. K1 is the nearby Masherbrum, much smaller at 7,821m (25,659ft).

Henry Haversham Godwin-Austen (1834–1923) was a lieutenant-colonel in the British Army who served on the Trigonometrical Survey of India, the Great Trigonometric Survey. His name was suggested for K2, which appeared to have no local name and still does not, but the Royal Geographic Society demurred, mindful of the controversy over the naming of Everest. 'Mount Godwin Austen' thereafter appeared on some maps, and it is still referred to by that name.

MOUNT LOGAN

The highest mountain in Canada at 5,959m (19,551ft). Located in Kluane National Park and Reserve in Yukon, it was given the name of Sir William Edmond Logan (1798–1875), founder of the Geological Survey of Canada.

MOUNT MCKINLEY

At 6,196m (20,327ft), this is the highest mountain in the USA and it is located in Alaska. If you ask the Alaskan State Board of Geographic Names, they will tell you that there is no such place as Mt McKinley, as they recognise the local Native American Athabascan tribe's name for the mountain which is Denali, or The Great One. The US National Board, however, still calls it Mt McKinley after President William McKinley (1843–1901). He was the Republican Party candidate for the US Presidential election in 1896 when a gold prospector, William Dickey, called for the mountain to be named after him in retaliation for the local silver miners asking for it to be named after Democratic candidate William Jennings Bryan who wanted a silver standard for currency, while McKinley was in favour of the gold standard.

Mt McKinley stuck, especially after he won the Presidency, was re-elected and was then promptly assassinated by the possibly insane anarchist Leon Frank Czolgosz. Many Americans would see it as a slight to McKinley's memory if the name was officially changed, but many Alaskans see it as an insult to local people that the name was changed in the first place.

There is a facebook page dedicated to the campaign to rename the mountain Denali as it is sacred to the Athabascan people. It points out that McKinley never set foot on the mountain, but, if we remove all the names of people who never visited places named after them, we would all get very lost. Read the arguments and make up your own mind.

MOUNT STANLEY

The highest mountain in both Uganda and the Democratic Republic of the Congo, on whose border it sits. It is the third-highest mountain in Africa, and is named after Sir Henry Morton Stanley (1841–1904), the Welsh-born explorer and journalist who 'found' David Livingstone – the Scot didn't consider himself lost – and said, 'Dr Livingstone, I presume?'

Stanley is a controversial figure in the Congo for his alleged treatment of native Africans, but there is no great campaign to change its name because the Congolese people call it Ngaliema in any case. The summit is also known as Pic

Marguerite or Margherita Peak after Queen Margherita of Italy, so named by the Duke of Abruzzi who led the first expedition to climb the mountain in 1906. A possible contender for the most eponyms associated with a geographical feature.

MURRAY RIVER

After the Mackenzie, this is the second-longest river named after an individual and also gets its name from a Scotsman, though he never went near Australia. The Murray and the Darling together form the longest river in Australia and the 15th-longest in the world at 2,375km (1,476 miles).

This is another case of brown-nosing by British explorers. Captain Charles Sturt named the river in 1830, not realising it already had a name – the Hume, after the father of explorer Hamilton Hume. Sturt named it after Sir George Murray, then Britain's Secretary of State for War and the Colonies, who also has Mount Murray in Australia named after him.

OWEN STANLEY RANGE

Captain Owen Stanley RN (1811–50) sighted and described the largest mountain range in Papua New Guinea in 1849 while surveying the west of the island. A Fellow of the Royal Society, Stanley had already carried out vital scientific work in the Antarctic before surveying Papua, still one of the world's last remaining wildernesses, a project which made him famous. He died a year later on the return journey, and the range was named after him.

ROSS SEA

Various members of the Ross family were arguably the greatest British explorers of the Arctic and Antarctic. The Ross Sea is named after James Clark Ross (1800–62) who discovered the sea during his expedition to the Antarctic from 1839 to 1943. The Ross Ice Shelf is also named after him, while Mount Erebus on Ross Island – the world's southernmost volcano – and Mount Terror in Antarctica are named after his ships.

Ross's uncle Sir John Ross (1777–1856) was a Scot who led his nephew on an Arctic expedition during which the younger man found the magnetic north pole on Boothia Island in 1831.

TASMANIA; TASMAN SEA

Abel Tasman (1603–59), Dutch explorer, was the first European to sail the sea between Tasmania and New Zealand. He found Tasmania while exploring the south-east coast of Australia, though Tasman first called the island Van Diemen's Land after a Dutch Governor-General of the East Indies, Anthony van Diemen, who commissioned the voyage. That name disappeared from use as Tasmania took over, but van Diemen is remembered in the name of the eponymous cape in New Zealand, Tasman having sailed on from Tasmania to become the first European to chart New Zealand.

VICTORIA FALLS

The world contains dozens if not hundreds of examples of places named after important people who never visited them, usually by explorers and cartographers wanting to curry favour with a patron, leader or monarch. The great age of British Empire exploration and development coincided with the reign of Queen Victoria (1819–1901), who thus has two States of Australia (Victoria and Queensland) and two State capitals of Canada (Victoria in British Columbia and Regina in Saskatchewan) as well as dozens of other places named after her. She even has an eponymous asteroid, 12 Victoria, discovered in 1850 by the British astronomer John Russell Hind. The Queen was the first living person to have an asteroid named after her, Hind saying the name was after the mythological 'Victory'.

There are a whole host of Victorias across the former British Empire and elsewhere – there are two Mount Victorias in New Zealand; Victoria Harbour in Hong Kong; Victoria is the capital of the Seychelles; Queenstown in South Africa was named after her; her name is also plastered across the UK where just about every sizeable town has some street or institution named after the mother of all empresses.

Whisper it in republican circles, but there is even a town in the USA named after her – Victoria in Virginia, a railroad 'planned' town founded in 1906.

The Queen reigns large over the map of Africa, too. The explorer John Hanning Speke named Africa's largest lake after her, but of all the many places named after the Queen, the most spectacular is Mosi-oa-Tunya, the Mist that Thunders, better known to us as the Victoria Falls.

More than a mile wide, the Falls carry the Zambezi River, where it forms the border between Zimbabwe and Zambia, through a series of gorges and cataracts, of which the largest, most famous and most photographed waterfall is in the first gorge. A bridge over the second gorge gives tourists a spectacular view of the Falls, which were given their name by the great Scottish missionary and explorer David Livingstone who was the first European to see them. There's the rub – Livingstone got there 'first' but only after many, many generations of Africans. They may be the Victoria Falls to Britons and most of the rest of the world, and perhaps curiously to the Zimbabweans, but in Zambia the Falls retain their name of Mosi-oa-Tunya, to which Her Majesty would no doubt have declared, 'We are not amused.'

WEDDELL SEA

James Weddell (1787–1834) did not come from a traditional background for explorers – his voyages to the Antarctic were in search of seals as he made his money from catching them for their skins and blubber. Looking for seals, he sailed further south than any man had done in 1823, and it would be 80 years before anyone went nearer to the South Pole. Though he died poor after his sailing career ended, Weddell enjoyed some fame during his life, and the sea and the Weddell Islands in the Falklands were named after him for his feats.

EPONYMOUS COUNTRIES

AMERICA

The entire continent is named after Amerigo Vespucci (1454–1512), an Italian merchant who sailed with Portuguese expeditions and who proved that the continent was much, much larger than originally thought and was certainly not

Asia as Columbus believed. He later became responsible for planning all Spain's voyages to the west.

How did America inherit his name and not that of Columbus? The explanation is complex, but after he wrote letters about his trips, signing himself 'Americus Vespucius' in Latin, the first widely available map to show the New World – a term he coined – showed the lands as 'Americas', the feminine form of Americus. The claims that the continent is named after a Bristolian merchant called Ameryke are extremely dubious. Fortunately, the mapmaker went with Amerigo's first name rather than his surname, or else we might be talking about the United States of Vespuccia.

BERMUDA

Another early transatlantic explorer was Juan de Bermudez (d. 1570), navigator and chronicler. He was captain of a Spanish vessel which discovered the island in the early years of the 16th century.

BOLIVIA

Simon Bolivar (1783–1830), the Great Liberator of Latin America, was actually from Venezuela, but his name was given to its neighbour in honour of his fight for freedom. Bolivar's name is also given to the boliviano, the currency of that country, and the bolivar fuerte is the currency of Venezuela.

CAMBODIA

Kambu Swayambhuva was a wise prince in India who sailed

east in prehistoric times to found the country which bears his name.

COLOMBIA

Christopher Columbus (1451–1506) was cheated; he 'only' had a country and not a continent named after him. There are many towns and cities which bear his name, however.

DOMINICAN REPUBLIC

The name comes from Santa Domingo, the first European settlement in the New World, named by Columbus's brother Bartholomew (1461–1515) after his favourite Saint, Dominic. With Haiti, it forms part of the island of Hispaniola.

EL SALVADOR

Named as such in the early 16th century by its first Spanish Governor, Pedro de Alvarado (d. 1541). The name is Spanish for 'the Saviour', Jesus Christ.

KIRIBATI

This is the local pronunciation of 'Gilbert', the islands formerly being named after Thomas Gilbert, the British captain who was the first European to reach them in 1788.

MARSHALL ISLANDS

Another place named after a British explorer, Captain John Marshall (1748–1819), seagoing colleague of Gilbert, who charted the islands.

MAURITIUS

Named in honour of Prince Maurice of Nassau (1567–1625), by sheer luck. The five Dutch ships which landed on the island only did so after being blown off course.

PHILIPPINES

King Philip II of Spain (1527–98) gave his name to the country thanks to explorer Ruy Lopez de Villalobos (1500–46).

SAUDI ARABIA

Imam Muhammad bin Saud (d.1765) was the founder of the House of Saud. The present kingdom, the third Saudi State, was established by his descendant Ibn Saud, known to his people as Abdul-Aziz bin Saud, who claimed almost the entire territory of the Arabian Peninsula by conquest over a 30-year period in the name of the Saud family. Saudi Arabia was formally established as an Islamic monarchy in 1932 and, since his death, only his sons Faisal, Khalid, Fahd and Abdullah have ruled the kingdom.

SEYCHELLES

After taking possession of the islands in 1756, the French East India Company named the islands in honour of Jean Moreau (1690–1761), a French politician who bought the Séchelles estate in northern France and became Moreau de Séchelles.

EPONYMS DERIVED FROM PLACES

ANGORA

Mohair from Angora goats and wool from Angora rabbits

are named after Angora, former name of Ankara, capital of Turkey, where both animals and Angora cats originated.

ARMAGEDDON

No, not a nightmare fantasy, but a real place. This synonym for the end of the world comes from the final battle between the forces of good and evil as predicted by many religions such as Christianity. It comes from Tel Megiddo, a small hill called Megiddo in present-day Israel where many battles were fought in ancient times and the predicted site of Armageddon. Given the violent and apocalyptic nature of the forthcoming Armageddon, one can only feel sorry for the inhabitants of nearby Megiddo, a small kibbutz.

BAYONET

The stabbing implement at the end of a rifle takes its name from Bayonne in France which was known for its production of long knives.

BIKINI

The two-piece swimsuit takes its name from the Pacific atoll in the Marshall Islands which was rendered uninhabitable for decades due to the 23 nuclear weapons tests that took place there between 1946 and 1958. The islanders were removed and paid compensation but many were contaminated by radioactivity. The bikini was launched a few days after the first test, and the name caught on because the suit had been 'split like the atom'.

COACH

Kocs is a Hungarian town west of Budapest whose 15th- and 16th-century wheelwrights specialised in carriages with a sprung suspension which Hungarian nobles found to be far more comfortable to travel in than existing vehicles. King Ferdinand III of Hungary (1608–57) made 'Kocs' carriages fashionable across Europe, and the House of Thurn and Taxis – no connection to taxi cabs – used them for the imperial postal service, so that the word about Kocs 'coaches' being faster and better spread everywhere. The word 'coach' still refers to a type of vehicle, while the other meaning of mentor or instructor comes from the sense that a leader conveyed students through a learning process.

COLOSSAL

The Colossus of Rhodes was one of the seven ancient wonders of the world. A huge iron and bronze statue of Helios, the Greek god of the sun, it stood over the town of Rhodes on the island of that name in the 3rd century BC and was destroyed by an earthquake in 226BC. It lay on the ground for hundreds of years, so we know for certain from historical reports that it was very big, more than 30m (100ft) high, hence the word 'colossal'.

DENIM

From 'serge de Nîmes', a sturdy cloth made in the French town of that name which was the original cloth used in jeans, another eponym which derives from the blue dye of Genoa – Gênes in French.

DUFFLE

The duffle coat takes its name from the Belgian town of Duffel near Antwerp. The coat was not invented there, but the Duffel cloth was the type most commonly used in their manufacture.

DOLDRUMS

When we say we are in the doldrums, we usually mean we are downbeat and listless, just like sailors and ships becalmed in the areas either side of the equator where winds often drop away. Technically, it is the Intertropical Convergence Zone, but that's a little too much of a mouthful when you're lacking in energy.

FRANKFURTERS

The adjective from the city of Frankfurt am Main in Germany is Frankfurter, and it was in that city that long, soft sausages became a speciality from 1852 when the local butchers started producing them.

HAMBURGERS

Hamburg Steak was the original name of the dish made from shredded beef usually mixed with spices which originated in Russia but was made famous in the German city. In the late 19th century, Frankfurters appeared in the USA courtesy of German immigrants, so 'steak' was dropped and 'hamburgers' arrived.

LABYRINTH

In Greek mythology, the original Labyrinth was a

convoluted building designed by Daedalus – the prototype of all engineers and architects – for King Minos of Crete to house the minotaur, the half-man, half-bull monster who was killed by Theseus.

LACONIC

The people of Laconia, the ancient Greek province which contained the city of Sparta, were famous for not saying very much, but saying it well.

MECCA

We describe a place as being a 'Mecca' when it is the centre of attention, which the city of Mecca in Saudi Arabia is at least five times a day for every Muslim. The holiest place of the Islamic religion is the place Muslims must turn towards when they pray.

PHILISTINE

Since Philistia no longer exists, calling someone a Philistine is usually an insult, unless that person really is ignorant and uncultured. The Philistines were the enemies of the Israelites and, since the latter wrote the Bible, they gave the Philistines a poor reputation. Goliath of Gath is the best-known Philistine, since the boy David felled him with a slingshot and cut off his head.

SODOMY

Also from the Bible, the sexual practice of sodomy takes its name from the city of Sodom where the local populace enjoyed that sort of thing, before they were all killed along with the citizens of nearby Gomorrah, who were also deemed to be pretty sinful, God raining down fire and sulphur upon the entire population.

SPA

Resorts, towns and baths which bear the name of spa are so called because of the town of Spa in Belgium, known for its curative waters as far back as the days of the Roman Empire, and called Espa in the local Walloon language.

SPARTAN

One of the most remarkable cities in the history of the world, Sparta was at the centre of the Laconia region of Greece. In order to maintain a formidable army, every male Spartan citizen could be called to arms, and proof of their military capability was the Battle of Thermopylae when 300 Spartans led by King Leonidas defied the Persian Army numbering tens of thousands.

Since every man was theoretically a soldier until the age of 60, a fierce discipline was practised throughout Sparta, including considerable frugality – money was not something a Spartan concerned himself with.

Hence, we use the word 'Spartan' for plainness and austerity. Despite its fame and military power, the strict citizenship laws made it inevitable that the population would decline and, in the centuries before the Roman Empire came along, Sparta just withered away. Yet Sparta was still admired by many people and there are towns named after it in many countries. The modern town itself is called Sparti, and was built from scratch on the site of ancient Sparta by order of

King Otto of Greece (1815–67). The present Spartans are very different from their ancestors and live happily in a quite beautiful town.

SYBARITE
Quite the opposite of Spartans, the people of Sybaris, an ancient Greek town located in the modern province of Cosenzo in southern Italy, were so wealthy and self-indulgent that their name became synonymous with pleasurable excess. But by the 6th century BC, the Sybarites were apparently so used to gluttony and good living that they forgot how to fight, and, when they went to war with the rival city of Crotona, the Sybarites were destroyed, and the river Carthis was diverted to sweep away any remnant of the luxurious city. A moral there, perhaps.

TUXEDO
A dinner jacket or suit in the USA is known as a 'tuxedo' or 'tux' from Tuxedo Park Country Club in New York State, whose wealthy and well-known members were the first Americans to wear the outfit regularly.

UTOPIAN
We use the word utopian largely in two ways – either to mean a perfect state or civilisation, or to mean an ideal that is impracticable. Thomas More used the Greek word for his fictional island in his eponymous book of 1516. Some of the ideas in *Utopia* suggest that More was not entirely serious, as the inhabitants kept slaves, anyone having sex before

marriage was sentenced to lifelong celibacy, and there were no lawyers because there was no need for laws – the joke being that More himself was a lawyer.

·3·

HONOUR BOUND

Names attributed by others to people involved with discoveries, inventions, creations and explanations of phenomena.

SCIENTIFIC ATTRIBUTIONS

ALGORITHM

Expressed most simply, an algorithm is a set of instructions that lead to the solution of a problem. The word has been in vogue for many years now, largely because of its use in computer science, where algorithms are ubiquitous in programming, for instance.

In true algorithm form, let's take a step-by-step approach to finding the derivation of the word.

Ancient humans learned to count; they used simple counting machines like an abacus to help them; along came Greeks like Euclid who wrote down the process of calculation; as with so much Greek lore, their scientific ideas were preserved to the east of the Mediterranean where a

Persian scholar called Muhammad ibn Musa al-Khwarizmi, working in the famous House of Wisdom in Baghdad in the 9th century, made advances such as codifying algebra and inventing the decimal point; his work was translated into Latin in the 12th century and became so influential in the West that his Latinised name – 'algoritmi' – was used to mean a calculating method.

It was most probably a mistake that people began using the word – recent research shows that the title of his translated seminal work, *Algoritmi de Numero Indorum*, was misunderstood, and people thought 'algoritmi' was the description of the methods rather than the name of al-Khwarizmi.

Islamic scholars tend not to get the credit they deserve in the western world, so mistake or not, it is surely satisfying that the man known as the father of algebra is given true credit in the word 'algorithm'.

AMPERE

The International System of Units, or SI Units, recognises just seven main units for measurement, though there are many more derived or supplemental units. Only two of the main units are eponymous: 'kelvin' (about whom more later) and 'ampere'. The latter word is often shortened to 'amp' and is the SI unit of measurement of electric current.

For the technically minded, the definition of ampere in one dictionary is 'that constant current which, if maintained in two straight, parallel conductors of infinite length, of negligible circular cross-section, and placed 1m apart in a vacuum, would produce between these conductors a force of 2×10^{-7} newton per metre'. We'll take their word for it.

The name was given to the measurement by scientists in honour of the French genius André-Marie Ampère (1775–1836), who was the first man to write down many of the basic descriptions of electromagnetism or electrodynamics, as he called it. He also predicted many developments in the field which could not be discovered during his lifetime as the experiments were simply not technically possible until later, and it is for that foresight that he was acknowledged by later scientists.

The man himself should be more acclaimed as a hero, since he overcame great personal unhappiness to produce his theories. His father was executed during the French Revolution, and his wife died young, which were just two of the reasons he had a long philosophical tussle over his Catholic beliefs. He is buried in Montmartre cemetery in Paris.

ARCHIMEDES SCREW

Yet another of those eponyms in which someone is claimed to have invented something when he possibly did not.

The pump which bears the name of the Greek mathematician and inventor is a device for lifting water from one level to another using a rotating screw. Archimedes, who was born around 287BC in Syracuse in Sicily – then a Greek colony – was said to have devised his screw pump in order to lift water out of the bilges of ships. It is one of several inventions he is credited with, although his work in mathematical theory is the foundation of his fame. He is the man who, having found the method for measuring density through water displacement – the Archimedes Principle – ran naked through the streets shouting 'Eureka', or 'I've found it!' One can only wonder what his fellow citizens thought he had found.

Archaeologists have found evidence that similar pumps existed in Egypt and possibly elsewhere in the Middle East prior to Archimedes. Intriguingly, Archimedes is supposed to have studied in Egypt as a teenager, so perhaps he saw one. There is no more ancient example, however, to beat Archimedes' undoubted claim to have invented a working screw pump.

His invention is still used across the world today, and a modern version was used to reclaim the land on which a lot of the Netherlands now stands.

The death of Archimedes is one of the best-known tragedies of ancient Roman history. During the siege of Syracuse around 212BC, Archimedes devised several weapons to keep the invading Romans at bay. The Roman commander, General Marcellus, was supposed to have been so impressed that, when his troops finally broke into the city and started butchering the populace, he ordered that Archimedes be spared so he could work for Rome. A soldier found him hard at work on some calculations, and so engrossed was Archimedes that he ignored the order to surrender, whereupon the enraged Roman killed him. A bit of an Archimedes screw-up, you might say.

BAKELITE

Now only seen in antique shops, Bakelite was the first completely synthetic plastic and is probably best remembered for its use in old telephones and radios. It was classed as a 'thermoplastic' and was highly prized because it could be mass-produced and was resistant to electricity and heat.

Bakelite was the creation of Leo Baekeland (1863–1944), a Belgian chemist and entrepreneur who emigrated to the USA in the 1890s. There he devised a new kind of photographic paper he called Velox, for which he became an instant millionaire when photography pioneer George Eastman paid him $1m for the Velox process.

His new wealth enabled Baekeland to conduct experiments in the relatively new field of synthetic materials, and he knew that real riches would come the way of anyone finding an insulator that could be manufactured cheaply for the fast-growing electrical industry. He devised this substance after three years of experimentation when he mixed phenol and formaldehyde in a controlled process. Baekeland announced his new invention to the world in 1909, almost two years after he had patented the process. On the day he filed the patent, Baekeland wrote in his diary: 'Unless I am very much mistaken, this invention will prove important in the future.'

That was true; Baekeland had created the first hard plastic that could be moulded into any shape. The name Bakelite was given an American-English spin by the inventor's marketing advisers, and he was happy with the spelling change as he was anxious not to damage any chance of it making him money.

Bakelite swept the world, and did indeed make Baekeland rich, although he had to settle for a Franklin Medal rather than a Nobel Prize for his invention of 'the material of a thousand uses' as his company called it.

Sadly, Baekeland became somewhat eccentric in later life and one later member of his family seemed to inherit mental disturbance – his grandson's wife Barbara Daly Baekeland, who was also possibly mentally ill, was murdered by her son Antony, who also stabbed and tried to kill his grandmother Nina Daly. Antony committed suicide in Rikers Island prison in New York in 1981.

There is a fascinating Bakelite museum in Williton in Somerset where many examples of the material of a thousand uses are preserved.

BEAUFORT SCALE

He is remembered today for wind speed, but in his lifetime Rear-Admiral Sir Francis Beaufort (1774–1857) was considerably better known as a cartographer and hydrographer, the man whose maps and charts of depths gave the Royal Navy the intelligence wherewithal to roam and rule almost all the known seas.

Born the son of an Irish Protestant clergyman and mapmaker who was one of the founders of the Royal Irish Academy, Beaufort's life was set on its course when he was just 15, as the ship he was travelling on in the service of the East India Company, the *Vansittart*, was wrecked due to the absence of a map of the shoals they were surveying. He determined that would not happen again.

Beaufort joined the Navy and, after several adventures, including the capture of a Spanish ship during which he was shot in the lung, he became a commander but had to retire from sea duty in 1812 after being wounded while tackling pirates in the Mediterranean.

His detailed maps and meticulous weather records led to him becoming chief hydrographer for the Navy, responsible for preparing the Admiralty Charts which were renowned for their accuracy in recording depths and coastline features.

Even before he retired from sea duty, he had devised his own scale for measuring winds. His suggestion for a wind scale was later adopted by the Admiralty. It originally had 13 described levels, listed 0–12, but was refined over the years to the present 13 wind speeds and sea heights in words that are now part of everyday language – flat calm to gale force, and hurricane.

Now here's where things become slightly less straight-forward – Beaufort's original scale was a different animal from the one we now know. He had devised it by researching previous work and making his own observations, but over the years the scale was written and edited by other naval personnel, creating the lyrical version we know today. Beaufort oversaw developments of his scale, and Captain Fitzroy, commander of *HMS Beagle*, was one of many sailors who wrote paeans of praise for him, suggesting it be named after him.

Beaufort went on to be one of the founders of the Royal Geographical Society and was lauded worldwide for the improvements he brought to mapmaking. Behind the respectable and respected personality lay a dark secret, however. In his coded diaries, Beaufort admitted to sleeping with his sister for three years in what is presumed to be an incestuous relationship. Well, he did keep details of practically everything else he did in his life, so why not that?

Beaufort cheese has nothing to do with him, it should be stated, as it hails from the Beaufort region in France. The Beaufort Sea north of Alaska, however, was indeed named in his honour.

BECQUEREL

You don't want to get too many becquerels – it is the unit by which radioactivity is measured, named after French physicist Henri Becquerel (1852–1908).

Already a distinguished professor, while working with uranium salts in 1896, he discovered natural or spontaneous radioactivity. He shared the 1903 Nobel Prize for Physics along with Marie and Pierre Curie. The cause of his death five years later was unknown, but he did suffer skin burns from handling radioactive material. The name was agreed by scientists years after his death.

BESSEMER PROCESS

This will confound trivia fiends everywhere. Henry Bessemer (1813–98) was not actually the first man to invent the process of mass-producing steel from pig iron. That honour should go to William Kelly of Eddyville, Kentucky, a qualified metallurgist who first demonstrated the technique of blowing air into molten iron to reduce its carbon content and make steel. There is unarguable evidence that he was making steel this way in the late 1840s and early 1850s, but apparently had no cash to exploit the invention. The wealthier Bessemer came along with his own similar process

– Kelly claimed it had been copied from his – and, crucially, the Englishman patented his in 1855, while Kelly only did so in 1857. The patent credited 'Bessemer' and 'Process', and an eponym was born.

BIRO

László Bíró (1899–1985) of Hungary invented the ballpoint pen which we usually refer to as a biro, but we should really render it as 'Biro', as it is a trademarked name. A journalist, Biro wondered if there was a way of putting quick-drying newspaper ink into a pen, and with his chemist brother Georg he eventually came up with the ballpoint in 1938. He sold the patent to French entrepreneur Marcel Bich, founder of the Bic group, in 1950, and that firm is still the world's largest manufacturer of biros.

BLUETOOTH

So how does a piece of contemporary wireless communication bear the name of a 10th-century king of two Viking nations? Harald Bluetooth (c.935–986) was King of Denmark who later joined his kingdom to that of Norway. He was responsible for spreading the gospel – a word meaning 'good news' – of Christianity across Scandinavia, so, when Swedish company Ericsson wanted a name that signified good news and good communications, they chose Bluetooth, for which the logo is derived from the runic symbols for H and B.

Old Harald clearly did not always communicate cleverly – his son, Sweyn Forkbeard, later King of England as well as Denmark and Norway, fell out with his father and Bluetooth was reportedly killed in battle against Sweyn.

BOOLEAN

George Boole (1815–64) was an English philosopher and mathematician who devised Boolean logic (Boolean algebra) which underpins the science of modern computing. Clearly, he could not have called Boolean logic in computing after himself – that would not be logical.

BRAILLE

Louis Braille (1809–52) was blinded as a small boy as the result of infection. He was given a scholarship which enabled him to become a fine organist, and a regular income allowed him to experiment with a system that used raised dots on paper to allow blind people to 'feel' their reading. By the time of his death, Braille was recognised as the foremost reading system for blind people in the world, and the name had been bestowed by public acclaim. He is buried alongside other French greats in the Panthéon in Paris, including two who are themselves eponymous – Marie Curie (see below), and Louis de Bougainville (see *Bougainvillea*, chapter 6).

BUNSEN BURNER

The one piece of laboratory equipment which everyone remembers from their schooldays is named after Robert Bunsen (1811–99), the German chemist who invented it along with his greatest student Gustav Kirchhoff. The two would go on to discover the elements caesium and rubidium.

CELSIUS

These days, people get confused between degrees Fahrenheit (see below) and Centigrade, so much so that people call the latter the Celsius scale, the formal name adopted by the scientific community in 1948. It would be a big mistake, however, to think they are exactly the same.

Anders Celsius (1701–44) was the Swedish scientist who devised the Centigrade scale – he divided the difference between the boiling and freezing points of water into 100 degrees. Here is the extraordinary thing – Celsius devised a scale which had 0 degrees as the *boiling* point for water, and 100 degrees as the *freezing* point.

Fortunately, his fellow Swede, Carl Linnaeus, came along and reversed things and, though he preferred Celsius's scale, Centigrade quickly became standard, as it was so much easier to understand a temperature scale divided into measurements of a hundredth rather than Fahrenheit's scale which used segments of 1/180th per degree.

To this day, of all the major countries, only the USA mostly retains the Fahrenheit scale as its principal measure of temperature.

CURIE

Polish-born Marie Curie (1867–1934) was one of the world's greatest scientists, winner of two Nobel prizes and, with her husband Pierre, the discoverer of polonium and radium. Her researches into radioactivity had a practical side – they took her to the trenches in the First World War where she drove a truck carrying X-ray equipment. She died of leukaemia, probably brought on by exposure to carcinogenic radioactive material.

The curie, named in her and Pierre's honour, is a measurement unit of radioactivity, but perhaps a greater tribute is the Marie Curie Cancer Care organisation, whose work is magnificent.

DAGUERREOTYPE

In France in the 1830s, chemist Louis Daguerre (1787–1851) created the first photographic development process a few years after his business partner Joseph Nicéphore Niépce made the world's first photograph, a heliograph. Daguerre's film process only allowed single pictures, but millions of daguerreotypes were made by enthusiasts, especially in France where the Government bought the patent from Louis and gave it 'free to the world', with the name of the inventor attached.

DARWINISM

Though the man himself would have been mortally embarrassed by his lasting fame, Charles Darwin (1809–82) is the only true progenitor of the bundle of theories concerning evolution that he first famously set out in his book *On the Origin of Species* which followed many years after his famous trip to the Pacific Ocean on *HMS Beagle*.

The adjective is Darwinian, and many people in the USA in particular view that as almost a swear word, so profound is their belief in creationism.

Darwin himself anticipated the clash between religion and science over his theory of natural selection, and it caused him great anguish. But he lived to see his work celebrated, and on his death he was given a State Funeral – a very rare honour for any Briton.

DAVY LAMP

Sir Humphrey Davy (1778–1829) could have been an English Romantic poet, but made the choice to devote himself to science, and he produced many discoveries in chemistry and physics that ensured his fame. In most history books, however, he is remembered for the simple but brilliant safety lamp that was used by miners and almost overnight made the coal pits of the world a safer place. The miners themselves called it the Davy Lamp, not least because the scientist never took out a patent or tried to make money from his invention.

DECIBEL

It should really be decibell, because this unit of measurement of the power of noise was named by its inventors at Bell Laboratories after their founder Alexander Graham Bell (1847–1922), the Scot who invented the telephone.

DIESEL

Rudolf Diesel (1858–1913) was a German engineer (though born in Paris) who devised his eponymous engine shortly after his compatriots Gottlieb Daimler and Karl Benz independently pioneered the automobile with the internal combustion engine. Diesel's early engines were risky – one exploded and nearly killed him – and were too large and cumbersome for cars, but achieved impressive power output and, after his death, diesel engines were devised and refined for just about every possible use. Given the modern obsession with biofuels, it is perhaps interesting that Diesel used peanut oil in one of his first engines, which were called diesels by the public, not the inventor.

His death was the greatest mystery about Diesel. He was on board a steamship heading for London for a meeting about building a new factory in England when he either fell or was pushed overboard. His body was found ten days later in the sea, but was already so badly decomposed that the fishermen who found him removed his personal effects and left the body to the deep. Sensational theories abounded that he had been killed by hitmen from the powers behind rival engines, or by German secret agents determined to prevent his secrets going to the British, or even that the body was not him at all and that he was trying to disappear. No proof of homicide or suicide has ever been found.

DOLBY

Dolby sound is all around us, and is a genuine product of British and American co-operation. Ray Dolby (b. 1933) was an American engineer who invented his audio reduction system in 1965 at his laboratories in London. He moved back to the USA and worked on many developments of his system. At first, the inventor wanted his system to be given a technical name, but he was persuaded to change his mind and attach Dolby Laboratories to the invention, and its use is now so widespread in film and music technology that Dolby has become a billionaire.

DOPPLER SHIFT OR EFFECT

If you stand at a railway station and listen to a train passing through, the noise as it leaves will be distinctly different from the noise as it approached you. This is the Doppler Shift or Effect, first conjectured by Christian Doppler (1803–53), an

Austrian professor of mathematics, physics and astronomy who published his theory about wave frequencies – sound or light or even water – varying according to the speed of the wave and the observer. It might seem obvious, but Doppler proved that his Shift had applications for observing light across the universe, and astronomers still use it in their calculations about galaxies.

FAHRENHEIT

The temperature scale named after Daniel Gabriel Fahrenheit (1686–1736) has fallen out of favour in most countries, except the USA. The man himself was thrust into a working life at an early age after his parents died from eating poisonous mushrooms. He was not only a clever student of engineering but also a trained glassblower who could make his own thermometers and barometers, which the public in Holland snapped up, along with the scale they soon called Fahrenheit.

FARADAY'S LAW (AND OTHER ATTRIBUTIONS)

The work of Michael Faraday (1791–1867) paved the way for the modern world to begin taking shape. The son of a blacksmith and largely self-taught, he came under the tutelage of Humphrey Davy, then the greatest scientist of the age. Faraday surpassed him, however. The English chemist and physicist was arguably the greatest experimental scientist of all time, as is proven by the many scientific laws and discoveries named after him. Of these, the most important is his Law of electromagnetic induction, which he defined in 1831. It's a bit complex for the layman, but here goes: 'The electromotive force induced in a circuit is directly proportional to the time rate of change of magnetic flux through the circuit.'

Take it from the experts that Faraday's Law, based upon his experimental discoveries, underpinned the development of electric machines and motors and began the electrical revolution.

Many other discoveries and theories flowed from Faraday's ever-questing mind, and were given his name – Faraday's Paradox, the Faraday Constant, the Faraday Cage and many more.

All were attributed to Faraday by other people, and the man himself was distinctly embarrassed by the fame he was given. For, in a situation rich with irony, the man whose name is plastered all over modern science never sought credit for his work, as to do so would have been contrary to his strictly followed Sandemanian Christian beliefs which emphasised modesty and plainness.

To the incredulity of Victorian Britain, before his death in 1867 at the age of 75, Faraday refused a knighthood and twice turned down the chance of being President of the Royal Society, then a far greater honour than it is now.

Michael Faraday, it seems, was a law unto himself.

FIBONACCI SEQUENCE

Take 0, add 1, you have 1. Add the two previous numbers, i.e. 1 and 1, and you have 2. Add 2 and 1, you get 3. And so on *ad infinitum*. This is the Fibonacci Sequence of numbers which for reasons unfathomable to lay people has excited arithmeticians and mathematicians since it was first written by Leonardo Fibonacci (c.1170–1250). He was also known as Leonardo of Pisa, and is best known for his hugely influential book *Liber Abaci*, the book which introduced the West to the Arabic numeral system.

GALVANISATION, GALVANISE

His famous experiments on dead frogs have been repeated in a million school physics classes, but Luigi Galvani (1737–98) of Bologna in Italy only discovered bioelectricity by accident – he was actually conducting a dissection to prove that a frog's testicles are in its legs, which they aren't. Until then, everyone thought nerves in man and animals were for distributing water to the muscles, but Galvani was fascinated by 'animal electricity' as he called it and thus proved that nerves were for carrying electrical messages. His rival Alessandro Volta (see *Volt; Voltage* below) suggested that this 'new' type of electricity be called galvanism, and the scientist's name has since been attached to the galvanisation process and other electricity-based activities.

DEGAUSS

When you degauss your computer, as you should do regularly, to remove unwanted magnetic fields, you are paying a sort of tribute to one of the greatest of scientists who was known as the Prince of Mathematicians.

A man with an intellect that ranged over a huge number of scientific fields, Carl Friedrich Gauss (1777–1855) was a German 'Renaissance Man', as comfortable in astronomy and statistical analysis as he was in pure mathematics. He was obsessional about his work – the story is told that, while in the middle of doing some calculations, he was informed that his sick wife was dying, only to reply, 'Tell her to wait a moment until I'm done.'

The Royal Navy invented and named degaussing to deal with magnetic mines in the Second World War.

GEIGER COUNTER

A device for measuring ionising radiation, and beloved of movie-makers who like noisy clicking machines in science fiction, it is named after Hans Geiger (1882–1945), a German physicist who first developed it with Ernest Rutherford and then vastly improved the apparatus with his fellow German Hans Müller, so that it should properly be known as a Geiger-Muller Counter. Geiger's work for the Nazis in the 1930s and 1940s in trying to develop a nuclear reactor has made his reputation questionable.

HEAVISIDE LAYER

When the musical *Cats* was first produced, most of the audience were intrigued, and probably did not have a clue as to what was meant by the 'Heaviside Layer', to which Grizabella ascends at the climax of the show. They thought it was some sort of reference to heaven and, in a way, that is correct, though the original author on whose works *Cats* is based never intended Heaviside Layer to mean Heaven.

The lyrics of the songs in *Cats* were based on the poetry of TS Eliot, and he undoubtedly knew what the Heaviside Layer is: the band of ionised gas situated between 60 and 90 miles above the Earth, which 'bounces' radio waves over the horizon.

British physicist Oliver Heaviside (1850–1925) predicted its existence in 1902, at the same time as American electrical engineer Arthur Kennelly (1861–1939) also made the same prediction, which is why in the USA and elsewhere the layer is sometimes known as Kennelly-Heaviside.

Heaviside was a largely self-taught genius of a mathematician and physicist who made huge advances in fields ranging from calculus to radio waves. Yet he received little recognition in his life, and did not profit from any of the scientific inventions that followed from his work. He became disillusioned and eccentric and died in relative poverty and obscurity in Devon.

At least he lived to see the Heaviside Layer proven, as English physicist Edward Appleton (1892–1965) devised experiments that comprehensively established where the Layer existed. Appleton made a career out of his work on the ionosphere, and was knighted and received the Nobel Prize for his work.

But is the Layer heaven? TS Eliot would have known all about the Layer as its discovery was a major news story in the 1920s. Yet he made only fleeting references to it in his work and letters, and it was *Cats'* composer Andrew Lloyd Webber and director Trevor Nunn who together made Heaviside Layer their analogy for heaven. In doing so, they made people think again about Heaviside, the scientist who never got the credit he deserved.

HERTZ; MEGAHERTZ

The SI unit of frequency, formerly known as 'cycles per second'. It was named by the scientific community after German physicist Heinrich Hertz (1857–94) who carried out pioneering work in electromagnetism.

JOULE

The SI derived unit of energy was named many years after his death in honour of James Prescott Joule (1818–1880), an English physicist who was also a trained brewer as his family owned a brewery in Salford, Lancashire. As a toiler in the beer trade, Joule suffered from intellectual snobbery among English scientists who dismissed his theories on heat and energy until William Thomson, Lord Kelvin (see below) began to take him seriously. There is a famous story that Joule conducted experiments by giving electric shocks to the family servants – one servant girl fainted, so Joule turned the shocking treatment on himself and his son.

KELVIN

The SI unit of measurement of temperature should really be called the Thomson, for that was the original name of Baron Kelvin (1824–1907), one of the most famous British scientists of the Victorian era whose name is attached to a list of scientific eponyms. Born in Belfast, but always associated with Glasgow where he became a professor at Glasgow University, Kelvin's genius ranged across a wide variety of scientific fields, as he constructed theories and made discoveries in everything from geology to thermodynamics. He was also instrumental in advising how the first transatlantic telegraph cable could be laid. His baronetcy was named after the River Kelvin, a tributary of the River Clyde in Glasgow, where his name is still revered.

LISTERIA

A genus of bacteria named after Joseph Lister (1827–1912),

the English surgeon who pioneered antiseptic surgery in Edinburgh and Glasgow. His name is also commemorated in Listerine mouthwash.

MACH NUMBERS

He was dead many years before the sound barrier was breached, but Austrian scientist Ernst Mach (1838–1916) was suitably posthumously honoured by having his name attached to the numbers that designate the speed of sound, Mach I being 761.2mph or 1,225km/h at standard sea level – the actual speed varies with temperature and air pressure.

Though he was better known as a philosopher in his time, Mach also conducted physics experiments such as photographing the shock wave of a bullet, just one of his many achievements.

MENDELIAN GENETICS OR INHERITANCE

Gregor Johann Mendel (1822–84) was the Austrian monk whose work on genetic inheritance in plants and insects would eventually rival the theories of Charles Darwin in importance in the field of evolution. Unlike Darwin, Mendel's work was not appreciated in his own lifetime, and its significance and the Mendelian name was not extant until the 20th century. He is now recognised as the father of genetic science.

MERCATOR PROJECTION

Almost every map of the world we look at today is the result of a deduction by Gerardus Mercator (1512–94), who was born in Flanders in what is now Belgium. His name is Latin for 'merchant', the family trade. He became a mapmaker who travelled widely in Europe and, as such, he attracted suspicion. Indeed, Mercator was at one point in his life facing the fate of being burned at the stake for heresy in those times of religious upheaval, but he survived to create the standard form of world map which is in use today.

MORSE CODE

If Samuel Morse (1791–1872) had had his way, he would have been remembered as a great painter, as he was indeed talented in that field, and also a great inventor as he pioneered the use of the long-distance electric telegraph. Instead, we remember him for the eponymous code which he probably didn't devise by himself – there is substantial evidence that his partner Alfred Vail played a bigger part in the invention.

Judged by our modern-day perspective, Morse was an anti-Catholic bigot and promoter of slavery, but he was also very generous and in many ways a sad person – as well as spending years in court defending his patents, the inspiration for his work in communications over distance was the fact that he didn't find out until too late that his wife was dying in Connecticut while he was in Washington.

NAPIER'S BONES

John Napier (1550–1617) was so clever that the public in his native Edinburgh thought he was a sorcerer. He discovered logarithms, and invented the abacus, later known as Napier's Bones, featuring the device called Napier's Rods. Napier University in Edinburgh bears his name.

NEANDERTHAL

What's the connection between a prehistoric cave dweller and the popular Christian hymn 'Praise to the Lord, the Almighty, the King of Creation'?

They are both linked by Neanderthals. This long-extinct species – though there are certain football clubs who appear to have preserved them in their support – of early Man is named after the Neander valley in Germany, which itself was named after Joachim Neander (1650–80). He was a famous Protestant preacher and hymn writer, who gave many sermons in the valley that was renamed after him by grateful local people. It was there that remains of Neanderthals were found in 1856.

NEWTONIAN LAWS

Newton's Laws of Motion and Universal Gravitation have guided science since the 17th century. Sir Isaac Newton (1642–1727) was arguably the greatest scientist in British history, whose work ranged across mathematics, physics, astronomy, optical science and even theology. He really did say that he was inspired to theorise about gravity because he saw an apple fall from a tree – it didn't hit him on the head as is often supposed.

There are numerous eponymous theories and objects derived from his name, with one that is still popular being Newton's Cradle, those annoying clicking metal balls that executives think make them look trendy when they actually look downright silly.

OEDIPUS COMPLEX

In the Greek myths, King Oedipus of Thebes inadvertently killed his father and married his widowed mother. Psychoanalyst Sigmund Freud used the story to give a name to his ideas that sons are in competition with fathers for the love of their mothers.

OHM

George Simon Ohm (1789–1854) was a teacher in his native Germany who started carrying out experiments on electrical current at the school where he worked in Cologne. His eponymous Law about current and resistance was rejected at first, but was later recognised for its fundamental importance. That and his other theories were recognised when the unit of electrical resistance was named after him.

PASCAL

Blaise Pascal (1623–62), a French philosopher and mathematician, is remembered by a host of eponyms, including the SI unit of pressure, the Pascal, his Law, Theorem, Triangle and the Wager. This last-named is the most intriguing, as it suggests that, if a rational person cannot be convinced of the existence of God, he or she should still 'wager' that God exists and live as though there is a God.

PYTHAGORAS' THEOREM

In the 6th century BC, the science of mathematics was already beyond the rudimentary stage in such places as India and Babylon until the Greeks came along and claimed credit for everything. Pythagoras was undoubtedly the first man to claim to be a philosopher, a lover of wisdom, and influenced Plato and therefore all western thought, but would himself have preferred to be remembered as the founder of a religion, Pythagorianism. Instead, he is recalled by the eponymous theorem about triangles which states that 'the square of the hypotenuse is equal to the sum of the squares of the other two sides of the triangle'.

RICHTER SCALE

Devised by Charles Richter (1900–85) in association with Beno Gutenberg at the California Institute of Technology, the Richter Scale, first introduced in 1935, measures the magnitude of earthquakes and earth tremors. Gutenberg's name was somehow forgotten in relation to the scale, but is remembered in the Gutenberg-Richter Law which applies to the magnitude and number of earthquakes in a given area.

ROENTGEN

Wilhelm Conrad Röntgen (1845–1923), whose name is usually rendered in English as Roentgen, was a shy, religious man and a scientific genius who discovered X-rays, otherwise known as Röntgen Rays, in 1895. His first 'ray' pictures of the bones in his wife's hand stunned the world, and he was awarded the first Nobel Prize for Physics in 1901. In time, Röntgen got his wish that the rays be known as 'X' rays, but his name is remembered in the Roentgen, the unit of measurement of radiation exposure.

SIEVERT

The SI derived unit for measuring radiation dosage is

named after Rolf Maximilian Sievert (1896–1966), a Swedish physicist who pioneered the use of radioactivity to treat cancer.

SMITHSONIAN INSTITUTION

The world's largest museum consists of 19 museums and galleries plus the USA's national zoo, with many of the facilities located in Washington. It is the largest research and education institution in America, yet, ironically, the man who provided the funds to found it never crossed the Atlantic. James Lewis Smithson (1764–1829) was a French-born British chemist and entrepreneur who was the illegitimate son of the Duke of Northumberland. He left his fortune to his nephew on condition that, if the nephew died childless, the money would be used to found 'an establishment for the increase of knowledge' in Washington – we still do not know why he chose the American capital. Fortunately for the USA, if not for the gentleman himself, the nephew passed away without leaving any children, and the Smithsonian Institution was born, the name being decreed by Smithson himself. Had he stayed with his original name – adopted to hide his illegitimacy – the Institution would be known as the Macie.

VENN DIAGRAM

We've all seen them, those overlapping circles which neatly show how things relate to each other. Unlike many eponymous discoveries or inventions that have come about by chance, the diagram was deliberately invented by English clergyman John Venn (1835–1923) to show a 'diagrammatic representation' of a theory or facts. Venn's other forgotten claim to fame was that he invented the first practicable bowling machine for cricketers to practise their batting.

VOLT; VOLTAGE
(adj. *Voltaic*)

Named after Count Alessandro Guiseppe Antonio Anastosio Volta (1745–1827), the SI derived unit for measuring capacitance, or the force or energy of electricity, is the volt, hence voltage. Born in Como, Italy, Volta was a teacher who experimented with gases – he discovered methane – before turning his full attention to electricity. He invented the Voltaic Pile, the forerunner of all electrical batteries, in 1800, and the Emperor Napoleon was so impressed with his work that the relatively low-born professor was created a Count.

WATT

If Scots seem to receive more mentions than most in this section, it's not because of the author's patriotism but rather the fact that Scotland possibly has produced a greater number of scientific geniuses than any other nation of comparable size.

One of these was James Watt (1736–1819), who famously 'invented' steam power after watching a kettle's steaming output. My fellow Scots will queue up to harangue me, but that story just isn't true.

For Watt did not invent the working steam engine – that achievement belongs to Thomas Newcomen of Devon in England (1664–1729). Whether or not he was inspired by the kettle in his aunt's house in Greenock, Watt certainly devised the separate condenser which massively boosted the power of steam and put the industrial revolution into overdrive.

He had many other inventions to his name, including an early photocopier, but it was for his work with steam that the unit of measurement of power was given his name by the British Association for the Advancement of Science, now the British Science Association, in the 19th century. The watt remains the Standard International (SI) unit for measuring power.

VAN ALLEN BELTS

In 1959, James Van Allen's name was reported to be 'ringing round the world' except for one rather large country – the USSR. The Van Allen Belts which bear his name are immense fields of radiation surrounding this planet, but at one time the Soviets just could not stomach the thought of having an American 'phenomenon' above them and they tried to change the eponymous Belts to 'Vernov', or at least Van Allen-Vernov Belts.

In the 1950s, astrophysicist Dr Van Allen was one of America's few homegrown scientists who was an expert on both rockets and what might be found in space.

Working out of the University of Iowa, he invented the 'rockoon', a rocket fired from a balloon which enabled him to carry out experiments at higher altitude than ever before. Later, along with colleagues William Pickering and the German-born scientist Wernher Von Braun, Van Allen devised the Explorer spacecraft which put America in the space race a year after Russia launched Sputnik in 1957. The early missions were part of the International Geophysical Year devised by Van Allen and some friends, the scientist always preaching a co-operative approach to science even at the height of the Cold War.

Based on results from his earlier experiments, Van Allen predicted that a belt of radiation would be found around the Earth if a geiger counter could be put into space. Proof of his theory came with the experiments of the third Explorer mission, and the world learned that it was surrounded by the Van Allen Belts, the name immediately given to the discovery by the acclaim of the international scientific community.

The exception was Russia, where Cold War mentality could not allow the American to be credited, so scientist Sergei Vernov was given the honour, before the Soviets backed down some years later in the face of incontrovertible proof that Van Allen was the discoverer. The Vernov Belts – just doesn't sound right, does it?

James Van Allen did so much more in the field of space exploration, although he never went into space himself. He gained many awards and decorations including being *Time* magazine's man of the year in 1960. He died in 2006, his name assured of immortality, a true 'eponymous' hero.

MEDICAL ATTRIBUTIONS

ACHILLES TENDON

Named after the Greek hero with the dodgy heel. There is evidence that the tendon had been so called from ancient times, but a 17th-century Dutch book of anatomy is the first written reference.

ADDISON'S DISEASE

Thomas Addison (1793–1860) was a brilliant English doctor and one of the first dermatologists. He described numerous diseases and conditions which bear his name but the best known is the eponymous disease which is caused by a deficiency of the hormones produced by the adrenal gland. Addison met a sad end, throwing himself into a basement area while suffering depression. Lurid newspaper accounts of his fatal plunge ascribed his mental illness to 'overwork of the brain'.

ALZHEIMER'S

Among the most feared and misunderstood of all diseases, dementia of this kind was first described by German psychiatrist Alois Alzheimer (1864–1915) in 1906 after years of studying the case of a woman in her early fifties, Auguste Deter, who showed the symptoms of senile dementia at her relatively young age. When she died, Alzheimer and colleagues were able to dissect her brain, thus proving the connection between her symptoms and the tell-tale changes to the brain's physical structures which cause the disease. As is the way with the medical community, his name was soon attached to the disease.

ASPERGER SYNDROME

This disorder in the autistic spectrum is named after Hans Asperger (1906–80), an Austrian paediatrician who first described the syndrome in 1944. He died before his breakthrough diagnosis was widely accepted from the 1980s onward.

BELL'S PALSY

The most common disease involving paralysis of the facial nerves, and caused by a range of conditions such as brain tumour or stroke. The best known of the several illnesses named after Charles Bell (1774–1842), a Scottish surgeon who described the condition and who made several other neurological discoveries. In his time, he was better known, however, for his paintings of the wounded at the Battle of Waterloo where he served as an army surgeon.

BILHARZIA

The other and more common name for schistosomiasis – a dreadful disease that afflicts millions in the Developing World – is named after German physician and pathologist Theodor Bilharz (1825–62) who first described the parasitic worm that causes the disease. Basing himself in Egypt, he often became carried away with his enthusiasm for his reports about intestinal parasites: 'These are a few leaves of a saga as wonderful as the best of *A Thousand and One Nights* if I could put it all together.' He caught typhoid fever from a visiting German duchess that he successfully treated, although he eventually died aged just 37.

BRUCELLOSIS

Infection by the bacteria Brucella was once rife in the western world, but is now thankfully rare. Major General Sir David Bruce (1855–1931), born in Australia of Scottish parentage, was instrumental in proving that the disease was linked to the bacteria which bears his name. Bernhard Bang (1848–1932), a Danish vet, discovered the genus of Brucella which infects cattle, which is why it is sometimes known as Bang's Disease.

CAESARIAN SECTION

As the legend suggests, Julius Caesar (100–44BC) was supposedly cut alive from his dead mother's womb. Except that he wasn't – his mother Aurelia Cotta lived into her sixties and was his adviser for many decades. The confusion comes from the writer Pliny the Elder, not always the most accurate of historians, who suggested that the family surname came from an ancestor who was *caeso* – a Latin nickname for someone cut from the womb. Pliny's version took hold and, when doctors finally managed to get the operation right about 1,500 years later, it was called after the Emperor. Yet another case of an undeserved eponym.

CREUTZFELD-JAKOB DISEASE

Hans Gerard Creutzfeld (1885–1964) and Alfons Maria Jakob (1884–1931) were two German neurologists who separately described cases of this fatal brain disease within months of each other in 1920 and 1921. CJD and variant CJD have become infamous as the product in humans of bovine spongiform encephalopathy, or mad cow disease.

CROHN'S DISEASE

Though several physicians from various countries gave descriptions beforehand, this intestinal disease is named after Burrill Bernard Crohn (1884–1983) who, with his colleagues Leon Ginzburg and Gordon Oppenheimer, described 14 cases that occurred in the USA in the 1930s. Dr Crohn, who practised medicine into his tenth decade, had the dubious honour of having the disease named after him simply because of the alphabet – his name appeared first on the jointly authored paper.

DALTONISM

Otherwise known as colour blindness, this condition was first described in scientific terms by John Dalton (1766–1844) who was best known in his lifetime for his scientific experiments and theories, of which the greatest was his atomic theory. He was born colour blind himself and, perhaps amazingly, no one had ever written a scientific description of the condition until Dalton decided to test out his own problem, hence Daltonism.

DOWN'S OR DOWN SYNDROME

John Langdon Haydon Down (1828–96) started his professional career as a research assistant to the great Michael Faraday. He became ill, and after a lengthy convalescence he entered medical school late and then switched entirely to the care of mentally ill people. His description of what was then known as 'mongolism' led to the condition being gradually renamed after him.

DUPUYTREN'S CONTRACTURE

Those people who have suffered from this baffling condition of ageing which affects the fingers, forcing them to turn in towards the palm – former Prime Minister Margaret Thatcher was one sufferer – will no doubt be interested to know that the man who first operated to cure the affliction was an expert in many medical fields. His name is applied to a dozen diseases and medical techniques, but he gained lasting fame from treating one of the least glamorous of all medical conditions – haemorrhoids.

Baron Guillaume Dupuytren was not born into the aristocracy – just as well for him, as he would have been guillotined during the French Revolution, at which time he was at school in Paris. The son of a struggling advocate, he decided to become a surgeon, and worked in a mortuary to pay his fees while living in poverty.

A determined student, he followed the methods of the then pre-eminent Scottish surgeon John Hunter, and after graduation he became renowned for his operating skills and for his research work in anatomy in particular, while his lectures soon attracted multitudes of students.

His surgical talents made him very wealthy and he became personal surgeon to Napoleon himself. It was for successfully treating the Emperor's infamous haemorrhoids that he first enjoyed international renown.

Though by all accounts he was a haughty, self-serving and greedy individual – 'the greatest of surgeons and the meanest of men', said one colleague – Dupuytren was undoubtedly a legendary figure in medicine.

The royal connections continued – King Louis XVIII made him a Baron, and he remained surgeon to the royal and wealthy of France until the stroke which preceded his death in 1835.

The curious Musée Dupuytren in Paris is also named after him as he bequeathed the money to establish this strange collection of anatomical specimens, many of them showing deformities and diseased organs.

EPSTEIN-BARR VIRUS

For once, a doctor did the decent thing and made sure his assistant got the credit for their joint work. English pathologist Sir Michael Anthony Epstein (b. 1921) discovered the virus in the 1960s with the aid of virologist Yvonne Barr (b. 1932).

FALLOPIAN TUBES

Gabriele Falloppio (1523–62) is best known for the eponymous tubes that are part of the female reproductive organs, but he also has a ligament and a facial canal (which carries an important nerve through the temporal bones in the skull) named after him.

One of the greatest of Italian anatomists, he is also credited with inventing the condom, or at least making it acceptable to wear, as he apparently had 1,000 men test it and none contracted syphilis, which was rife at the time.

GRAVES' DISEASE

The Irish-born surgeon Robert James Graves (1796–1853) was a polymath and a talented amateur painter – he was a friend of JMW Turner – who revolutionised the way that surgeons dealt with patients as he encouraged personal interviews to check on symptoms. He co-founded the Dublin School of Medicine and, among other achievements, he invented a second hand for pocket watches, although he didn't patent it.

His description of overactivity in the thyroid gland led to the disease being given his name, though it bears different names in different countries as several physicians researched it at the same time.

HEIMLICH MANOEUVRE
Dr Henry Jay Heimlich (b. 1920) is an American physician whose name is attached to the abdominal thrust used to stop a person choking. The actual invention of the manoeuvre is disputed, but Heimlich claimed it first. He also invented the Heimlich valve used in draining fluid from the chest.

HIPPOCRATIC OATH
The vow made by most doctors – some medical schools do not impose it – concerning the sanctity of life and professionals' morally correct approach to medicine. All current oaths derive from the original written by the sage Hippocrates who lived in Greece in the 5th and 4th centuries BC and who practised medicine and, more importantly, wrote about it in works which have survived to this day.

HODGKIN'S LYMPHOMA
Named after Thomas Hodgkin (1798–1866), the British pathologist who first described it in a paper of 1832. It was forgotten about until 1865, when Dr Samuel Wilks, later knighted, gave a fresh description and named it after Hodgkin.

HUNTINGTON'S CHOREA OR HUNTINGTON'S DISEASE
An inherited disease which causes dementia and physical

disorders. Although several doctors had attempted descriptions before, the American physician George Huntington (1850–1916) studied its hereditary aspects and first gave the fullest description, so earning the 'honour' of having it named after him.

ISLETS OF LANGERHANS

Sufferers of diabetes are usually best placed to know about probably the most strangely named part of the human body. They are the areas of the pancreas which store the cells that produce a variety of hormones, including insulin. They were discovered by German pathologist Paul Langerhans (1847–88) who also discovered the type of cells in human skin which also bear his name. Tragically, Langerhans contracted tuberculosis, possibly as a result of his work as a pathologist, and had to give up his research work at the height of his career before dying of complications of the disease.

KAPOSI'S SARCOMA

Due to its prevalence among people with AIDS, this form of skin cancer has become infamous. It was originally described by Hungarian dermatologist Moritz Kaposi (1837–1902).

LOU GEHRIG'S DISEASE

One of the few diseases named after a famous sufferer rather than the medical person discovering or describing the illness. It is known to doctors as Amyotrophic Lateral Sclerosis (ALS), an invariably fatal form of motor neurone disease. Lou Gehrig was one of America's greatest baseball players, known as 'The Iron Man' for his incredible feat of playing in 2,130 consecutive games for the New York Yankees. He had to retire at the age of 36 after contracting the disease which claimed his life two years later.

In America and many other countries, ALS has been known as Lou Gehrig's Disease since the film of his life, *Pride of the Yankees*, starring Gary Cooper and Babe Ruth himself, came out the year after Gehrig's death.

MESMERISM

Hypnotism, by another name, the eponym deriving from Franz Mesmer (1734–1815), a German physician who did not actually invent 'mesmerism' but suggested that there was a force called 'animal magnetism', although that term is misleading – magnets were not involved, and it took other experts to suggest that hypnosis was achieved by stimulating the imagination.

MÉNIÈRE'S DISEASE

Prosper Ménière (1799–1862) was the French physician who, in 1861, first described labyrinthine or inner-ear vertigo which is such a prevalent feature of the disease named after him.

NICOTINE

When an obscure French ambassador to Portugal in the 16th century sent some tobacco seeds to Paris, he could not have known that he would end up giving his name to a substance which some people consider to be a source of pleasure while others deem it an addictive poison which should be banned worldwide.

Jean Nicot de Villemain had been given tobacco seeds as a gift and had grown the plants in the garden of the French embassy in Lisbon. He already knew that tobacco (the name probably derived from the island of Tobago) was prized for its euphoric qualities as several explorers had come back from the New World imitating the indigenous people by happily smoking the herb. Tobacco was already used in Portugal to treat various medical ailments, and Nicot de Villemain became convinced of its efficacy and spread the word far and wide, and indeed its nickname was 'the Ambassador's Herb'.

Nicot de Villemain's seeds grew into tobacco plants at the Royal Court and soon they were seen as luxury items signifying wealth. While almost every other country in Europe cracked down on the 'heathen herb', the French persisted with their early Gauloises and the habit spread.

Two centuries later, when Swedish naturalist Carl Linnaeus was carrying out his great work of naming species, he called the tobacco plant *nicotania tabacum* in recognition of the ambassador's role. In 1828, while still students at Heidelberg University, two German scientists – Wilhelm Heinrich Posselt and Karl Ludwig Reimann – succeeded in isolating the active ingredient of tobacco and they named it 'nicotine'. So, if you are a user of the weed, next time you're drawing on a cigar or cigarette, remember to thank the ambassador.

PAP SMEAR

The test used to check for cervical cancer is named after the Greek doctor Georgios Nicholas Papanikolaou (1883–1962) who invented it. It seems incredible now, but it took him many years to convince medical colleagues that the Pap smear worked, and of course it is now the worldwide standard test.

PARKINSONISM; PARKINSON'S DISEASE

It is not often recognised that Parkinsonism is the correct collective noun which covers a whole range of illnesses whose common symptoms include tremor, slow movement and stiffness. Some 85 per cent of cases of Parkinsonism are the result of Parkinson's Disease.

One of the most feared afflictions of our age, this awful disease bears the name of a quite remarkable man who led a colourful life. James Parkinson was a Londoner, the son of a surgeon, who studied medicine and eventually took over his father's practice.

We know a lot about Parkinson, even what he was like as a person. The *Oxford Dictionary of National Biography* contains a description by a contemporary. He was 'rather below middle stature, with an energetic intellect and pleasing expression of countenance, and of mild and courteous manners'.

In the latter years of the 18th century, Parkinson became a political agitator, campaigning for reform on a host of issues such as voting rights that brought him into conflict with the Government of the day. At one point, he was even questioned about his alleged involvement in a plot to kill King George III. He was entirely innocent, fortunately.

As if surgery and social reform were not enough, Parkinson took up paleontology, and was one of the first Englishmen to write a scientific work on fossils. He embraced geology as well, all before writing his greatest work, *An Essay on the Shaking Palsy*, in which he gave descriptions of six people with the disease he called '*paralysis agitans*'. Though the disease has been known since antiquity – descriptions can be found in the Bible – according to the website of the Parkinson's Disease Society, this work of 1817 established the disease 'as a recognised medical condition'.

James Parkinson died in 1824, and 18 years later the French doctor Jean Martin Charcot, known as the father of modern neurology, along with his colleague Alfred Vulpian, revisited Parkinson's research and added some symptoms which they had observed. Crucially, Charcot realised the significance of Parkinson's original work and gave him the credit by naming the disease after the Englishman.

POTT'S FRACTURE; POTT'S DISEASE

Sir Percival Pott (1714–88) was an English surgeon who fell off his horse and broke his lower leg. The fracture was so bad that the leg was about to be amputated when Pott decided to try to save it with the help of his former tutor, Edward Nourse. Pott's leg survived and, perhaps unsurprisingly, Pott took great interest in bones and fractures afterwards, and his description led to the injury being named after him. He also described a tubercular infection of the spine, leading to the disease being named after him.

Yet his greatest work, which is still a subject of debate and sometimes court cases even today, was to prove that cancer could originate from outside the body, caused by carcinogens in the environment. He proved that by means of a rather unconventional and unpleasant test – by examining the scrotums of chimney sweeps. His sampling showed that the form of cancer which affected sweeps was caused by soot entering into their skin at a very vulnerable area.

PROTEUS SYNDROME
One of the world's rarest and, thanks to the film *The Elephant Man*, one of the most famous of all congenital disorders that was only described and named in 1979. The uncontrolled growth of bone and skin is named after the Greek sea-god Proteus who could change his shape. Its cause, and a cure, are still to be found.

RAYNAUD'S PHENOMENON; RAYNAUD'S DISEASE; RAYNAUD'S SYNDROME
This extraordinarily obvious illness in which the blood supply to the hands is affected with severe discolouration and sometimes devastating results is named after French doctor Maurice Raynaud (1834–81) who described the disease in his doctoral thesis while still only in his twenties.

RORSCHACH TEST
A form of psychological test which uses blotted ink shapes to measure unconscious reactions, it was devised by the Swiss psychoanalyst Hermann Rorschach (1884–1922) in 1921. He did not live to see his fame, as he died less than a year after his inkblot theory was published.

ST VITUS' DANCE; SYDENHAM'S CHOREA
Named after St Vitus, a young boy martyred by the Romans in Italy around 300AD, whose cult involved dancing in front of his statue. The alternative eponym derives from Thomas

Sydenham (1624–89), the English physicist who first described it.

SALK VACCINE

The polio vaccine was developed by New York-born Jonas Salk (1914–95) in the early 1950s and, after the announcement in 1955 that the vaccine was safe – Salk tested it on himself and his family – overnight he became the world's most famous medical scientist.

SALMONELLA

Nothing to do with fish, the genus of bacteria which is the cause of many food illnesses was named after the American veterinary pathologist Dr Daniel Elmer Salmon (1850–1914) after it was discovered in his laboratory by his research assistant Theobald Smith (1859–1934).

TOURETTE'S SYNDROME

Famous French neurologist Jean-Martin Charcot (1825–93), who has at least 14 eponymous but less famous medical conditions named after him, bestowed the eponym on this illness in honour of his protégé Georges Gilles de la Tourette (1857–1904). Tourette went on to become a neurologist himself, and suffered at the hands of a female patient who ended up shooting him in the head. He then went on to develop mental illness – but not Tourette's.

WEIL'S DISEASE

Also known as leptospirosis and called several other names, it was first described by German physician Adolf Weil

(1848–1916) in 1886, the year he caught tuberculosis and permanently lost his voice. The Adolf Weil motocross bike is named after another gentleman of the same name, the champion German motorcyclist who died in May 2011.

RELIGIOUS, POLITICAL AND PHILOSOPHICAL ATTRIBUTIONS

A small selection of 'isms' and other definitions. Interestingly, not one of these words was coined by the instigator of the idea or concept.

AMISH

Jakob Ammann (c.1656–1730) was the leader of a faction which split from the Mennonite congregation of Anabaptists, a reformed Protestant Christian denomination based mainly in Switzerland. Following the schism, the Amish Mennonites largely emigrated to the USA where there are now more than 200,000 in congregations in more than 20 States plus Ontario in Canada. Ammann's personal strictures about a disciplined approach to Christian observance are still the guiding principles of a faith which emphasises plainness in everything, and shuns modern technology.

BUDDHISM

Siddhartha Gautama Buddha (c.563–483BC) was the founder of Buddhism, a philosophy and religion which emphasises the path to enlightenment or awakening – Buddha means 'awakened one'.

Just as there are different varieties of Buddhism, so there

are different accounts of Siddhartha's life, but it is agreed that he was a prince of a kingdom, probably in what is now Nepal, who left the royal court to become a teacher and preacher. Unlike many monks of his time, the Buddha did not preach or practise an ascetic way of life.

That he put on weight in later life is attested to by the many statues that show him with a middle-aged spread. Traditionally, the Buddha is always portrayed with a serene countenance.

CALVINISM

John Calvin (1509–64) was a French theologian who thought that the Roman Catholic Church had moved away from the teachings of Jesus Christ (see below) and, influenced by Martin Luther and others, he started to preach radical reforms. It nearly cost him his life in the early backlash against the reformers, but he eventually made his home in Geneva where he preached a more radical form of Protestant Christianity which influenced preachers such as the Presbyterian Scot, John Knox, and the Puritans of England.

CHRISTIANITY

The religion begun by Jesus Christ, who lived and preached in what is now Israel from around 5BC to sometime between 24 and 30AD. His teachings about loving your neighbour as yourself, turning the other cheek to an opponent and caring for the poor, among others, remain revolutionary.

CONFUCIANISM

Shortly before the ancient Greek philosophers struggled to comprehend the world around us, over in China, Confucius

(551–479BC) had it all worked out. Known in his lifetime as Kong Qiu or Zhong Ni, Confucius was descended from nobility but was born and raised in poverty, working as a shepherd before he found his eventual career as an administrator in the state of Lu. He devised a system of philosophy and ethics which emphasises self-improvement and social harmony, and which came to dominate the culture of a large part of south-east Asia.

GERRYMANDER

One of those eponyms which people tend to think derives from someone's name – but who on earth was Mr Mander?

The answer is that there was no Mr Mander. The verb 'to gerrymander', meaning to fix the boundaries of an electoral district with a view to winning more votes for your party, comes from Governor Elbridge Gerry (1744–1814) who authorised the redrawing of the district boundaries in Massachusetts in 1812. Interestingly, Governor Gerry's name was pronounced with a hard 'g' as in get, unlike the 'g' in gerrymander, but that didn't stop his name being attached to the corrupt practice.

The local paper, the *Boston Gazette*, ran a cartoon apparently showing that one of the new, bizarrely shaped districts resembled a small dragon, or salamander. They called the creature 'The Gerry-Mander', and so outrageous was the 'gerrymandering' that the Governor's infamy spread across the USA and the name stuck.

HANSARD

The record of the proceedings of the Houses of Parliament in printed form has been known as *Hansard* since the mid-

19th century. It is another eponym which does not recognise the creator of the activity, for that was not Thomas Curson Hansard (1776–1833) but William Cobbett. It was Cobbett, a journalist, who started publishing weekly records of parliamentary debates in 1800, almost 30 years after another journalist and MP, John Wilkes, had won the right for newspapers and magazines to publish the proceedings in Parliament – no doubt there are still some politicians who wish their speeches, or lack of them, had remained secret.

Some 12 years after he started his weekly accounts, Cobbett went bust and had to sell his business to his printer, Thomas Hansard.

Hansard later put his name on the title page, and his sons expanded the business after his death. Gradually, *Hansard* gained the support of Parliament and became the 'paper of record' for the Houses of Commons and Lords.

Many other countries, mostly English-speaking and members of the Commonwealth, have their own *Hansards*. None has a *Cobbett*.

JACOBITE

Followers of the Stewart King James II of Great Britain (James VII of Scotland) (1633–1701) and his son and grandson, James Francis Edward, the Old Pretender, (1688–1766) and 'Bonnie Prince' Charles Edward, the Young Pretender (1720–88), were known as Jacobites, from Jacobus, the Latin word for James. Jacobitism emphasised the Stewart claim to the throne through the hereditary principle, religious liberty and also the divine right of kings to rule. The Jacobite cause was extinguished at Culloden Moor near Inverness on 16 April 1746, in the last pitched battle fought on British soil. Even today, the place has a desolate, melancholy air.

LENINISM

Vladimir Ilyich Lenin (1870–1924) was a bourgeois lawyer who became a political radical, not least because his brother Aleksandr was executed by the State for his involvement in a failed attempt to assassinate Tsar Alexander III. His interpretation of Marxism made the proletariat supreme, as long as they were led by a professional revolutionary vanguard, i.e. Lenin and his followers.

LUDDITES

Ned Ludd may or may not have been the Englishman in the late 18th century who reportedly smashed up two knitting machines that were taking away people's jobs, inspiring a rash of such incidents by people who came to be called Luddites. The trouble is, no one can find any trace of Ned being a real person, but he is certainly legendary.

LUTHERANISM

The denomination of Christianity which most closely follows the teachings of Martin Luther (1483–1546), a priest and doctor of theology, who famously and courageously defied Church law to become the founder of the Protestant Reformation.

MALTHUSIANISM

The Reverend Thomas Robert Malthus (1766–1834) was the son of an English gentleman, Daniel Malthus, who had interesting friends, such as the Swiss philosopher and writer Jean-Jacques Rousseau and the Scottish philosopher and historian David Hume, who both influenced young Thomas. Malthus was a brilliant student at Cambridge, and it is interesting to speculate that, had he not been born with a cleft palate and hare lip, he might have moved into politics. As it was, he became a clergyman, but continued with his theorising on new sciences such as demographics and economics. His writings were hugely influential, and are still discussed by economists and philosophers.

Malthus' most famous theorem was that 'the increase of population is necessarily limited by the means of subsistence', meaning that the human species should not increase its numbers beyond a sustainable level – as a good clergyman, he preached 'restraint' as a way of achieving sustainability. Two centuries later, the human experiment has yet to prove him right or wrong.

MAOISM

The teachings of Mao Zedong (1893–1976) guided the Chinese Communist Party until long after his death. The principal tenets were that the people needed to make war, militarily and culturally, to achieve revolution, and that the class struggle would never end – many millions died in Mao's campaign to change China.

There are Maoist parties in several countries, including Nepal, where the Communist Party has played the leading role in the country's political transformation in recent years.

MARXISM

Since it has been the creed of revolutionaries for more than a century, it is almost forgotten how revolutionary Marxism actually was.

At a time when political philosophy was the territory of supporters or opponents of the teachings of such varied personalities as Thomas Malthus, Charles Darwin, Adam Smith, Jeremy Bentham, John Stuart Mill, Arnold Bennett and John Ruskin, to name but a few, along came Karl Marx (1818–83) and his colleague Friedrich Engels and blew the whole polite debate to hell in a handcart.

Karl Marx changed the world. The reverberations of his teachings are felt to this day, even if most of the states that adhered to his theories are long gone.

After years of study and journalism, with Engels he wrote *The Communist Manifesto*. It was published in 1848, the Year of Revolutions, and nothing has ever been quite the same since, though in fact it took several decades for Marxism to 'take off' – when revolutionaries like Lenin and Trotsky formalised his thoughts into a genuine international class struggle.

Marx took his philosophy further by coming to England from his native Germany in 1849 during the height of Victorian industrialisation and analysing the situation of the workers. He concluded they were getting a very raw deal, and came up with his theories of class differences, exploitation and alienation that are influential to this day, and which were expressed in his dense, thorough and highly revolutionary masterpiece, *Das Kapital*, published first in 1867.

Marx was convinced he had produced the perfect political philosophy which, if adhered to in the fullest, would cause the world revolution which he had forecast. For the rest of his life, he would berate any follower who deviated from the master's word.

Yet, like almost all philosophers, and just like great religious figures – for instance, Jesus Christ and the Prophet Mohammed – what Marx wrote and taught was intrinsically problematic and has been open to differing interpretations ever since. From the outset, other thinkers spoke and wrote of Marxism, so that the man himself was once able to say, 'I am not a Marxist.'

As the *Encyclopaedia Britannica* states: 'The term Marxism is used in a number of different ways. In its most essential meaning, it refers to the thought of Karl Marx, but it usually extends to include that of his friend and collaborator Friedrich Engels.' The encyclopaedia goes on to detail the most important forms of Marxism, but in truth there have been dozens, adapted by self-proclaimed revolutionaries across the globe.

His most famous diktat was 'from each according to his abilities, to each according to his needs', and if the followers of Marxism had stuck to that simple creed … well, who knows what might have happened.

Marx spent the latter half of his life in London and is buried in Highgate Cemetery, as are writers George Eliot and Douglas Adams, the actor Sir Ralph Richardson and comedian Max Wall.

MCCARTHYISM

Seldom can a US senator have started out as such a hero and ended a zero with his name transformed into another word for state bullying and the casting of false aspersions. Joseph Raymond McCarthy (1908–57) was the Republican senator for Wisconsin who rose to fame by voicing fears of Communist infiltration of many levels of the American Government. In the rabid anti-Communist atmosphere of the 1950s, McCarthy was soon able to engage in a legal witch-hunt using Senate committees to start a wholesale investigation into allegations, spurious or otherwise, of people's past links with left-wing causes. His own reckless intimidation of witnesses and frequent making of unfounded allegations saw the public turn against him, and he was censured by the Senate, after which he turned to drink and died of liver disease.

MONROE DOCTRINE

First decreed by President James Monroe (1758–1831) in 1823, the United States of America declared that it would no longer tolerate European nations interfering in its business, and likewise the USA would not intervene in European issues. It remains a powerful concept in American politics. Monroe was the fifth President and last to serve in the War of Independence during which he was badly wounded. He died on 4 July, American Independence Day.

MOSAIC LAW

The guiding philosophy and legal precepts of Judaism were written by Moses in the 14th century BC as he led the Israelites out of Egypt.

MUGGLETONIAN

Lodowicke Muggleton (1609–98) was an English tailor who at the age of 41 decided he was one of the two prophets foretold in the Book of Revelation. The other was John Reeve, and together they founded the Christian sect that became known as Muggletonians.

RASTAFARIAN

The Rastafarian religious culture is named after Ras Tafari, one of the names of Haile Selassie I, Emperor of Ethiopia, also known as Abba Tekel, Tafari Makonnen and Talaqu Meri (1892–1975). Many Rastafarians believe he was the reincarnation of Jesus Christ.

REAGANOMICS

He may have been a figure of fun to many people outside the USA with his folksy ways, but history is already beginning to judge President Ronald Reagan (1911–2004) as one of the greater holders of the office, especially because of his remarkable contribution to ending the Cold War.

He began his Presidency in 1981 talking about beating Soviet Communism everywhere and ended it by embracing Mikhail Gorbachev and helping the reform movements in Eastern Europe.

The former screen actor's conservative philosophy on economics was not something he had to learn from a script. It is often forgotten that Reagan earned a degree in economics and sociology at Eureka College, Illinois – whisper it, but he was even a bit of a rebel there – before he hit Hollywood.

As President, and influenced by the same philosophy which guided Prime Minister Margaret Thatcher, Reagan set out to cut taxes, reduce government spending and red tape, and control the money supply to combat inflation. This draft of measures became known as Reaganomics, and, by the time he left office in 1989, the American economy had undoubtedly improved, although there is still some debate as to whether Reaganomics helped or hindered that process.

What cannot be doubted is Reagan's personal courage. He survived would-be assassin John Hinckley's bullet and, after he left office, took the brave decision to admit he was suffering from Alzheimer's Disease.

STALINISM

The philosophy, such as it was, of Joseph Vissarionovich Stalin (Ioseb Besarionis dze Jugashvili) (1878–1953), who turned the Marxist revolution in Russia into a hugely centralised bureaucracy which was effectively a dictatorship. Key elements of his version of Marxism were five-year plans, the cult of (his) personality, the aggrandisement of the Soviet State, the persecution of religion and the refusal to countenance opposition which led to millions being imprisoned and killed. He did lead the Soviet Union to beating Nazi Germany on the Eastern Front, but even that came only after a previous non-aggression pact with Hitler and then led to the creation of the Soviet-dominated Warsaw Pact.

TAMMANY HALL

A by-word for political corruption, the Tammany Societies began in Philadelphia in 1772 with the best of intentions, namely to promote brotherhood and charity with almost Masonic rituals based on the perceived activities of Native Americans – hence their meeting places being called 'the Great Wigwam' and the local leader entitled 'the Grand Sachem'.

The name Tammany was an elision of Tamanend (c.1628–1698), chief of a tribe in Delaware who made peace with the original English settlers and became renowned for his wisdom. Legends sprang up about his nobility, and his fame was so great that he was called Saint Tammany, the Patron Saint of America. A statue of him was erected and still stands in Philadelphia.

Sadly, the people who adopted his name did not always live up to his reputation. The biggest and eventually most infamous Tammany Society was founded in New York in 1789. It soon became active in politics, and, when Tammany Hall was built in 1830, it became a centre for intrigue and power-dealing within the Democratic Party.

Throughout the 19th and early 20th centuries, the Hall was the most powerful force in New York politics, leading to accusations of large-scale vote-rigging and corrupt practices.

Although it was originally open to all immigrants, Tammany Hall became dominated by Irish factions. Despite a succession of scandals, it still kept up the appearance of a 'friendly' Tammany Society until its power waned away and it all but ceased to exist in the 1960s.

THATCHERISM

There are certain parts of the UK where her name is still reviled. Margaret Hilda Thatcher (b. 1925), now Baroness Thatcher, was Prime Minister of the United Kingdom from

4 May 1979 to 28 November 1990, during which time she was leader of the Conservative Party, a post she gained on 11 February 1975, after defeating former Prime Minister Edward Heath. Classed as a right-wing Conservative, she was an ideologue whose beliefs in a free market economy, personal responsibility, curbing trade unionism and privatising state assets, and a hawkish approach to international affairs including confronting the Soviet Union, became known as Thatcherism and influenced Reaganomics (see above). How influential is she now? Google the word Margaret and see whose name comes up first.

TROTSKYISM

Marxism interpreted by Leon Trotsky (Lev Davidovich Bronshtein) (1879–1940), a leader of the Russian Revolution who was assassinated in Mexico by order of Joseph Stalin. The theory of permanent revolution is the best known of Trotsky's ideas, which are often cited as the most left-wing of political philosophies.

WESLEYAN

Relating to the religious beliefs and form of Christianity first espoused principally by John Wesley (1703–91) and also his brother Charles, the English clerics who are known as the founders of Methodism.

ZOROASTRIANISM

'*Also sprach Zarathustra*' … 'Thus spake Zarathustra'.

One of the most famous phrases in the German and English language, they are the opening words of the title of a philosophical novel by Friedrich Nietzsche. The book features the prophet Zarathustra, but, in Nietzsche's imagination, it is merely the name he borrows from the real man, known in English as Zoroaster, the founder of the religion Zoroastrianism.

We know very little for definite about Zoroaster. He was almost certainly Persian (modern-day Iranian) and lived somewhere between 1700BC and 500BC, though most expert scholars think he was extant around the 11th or 10th century BC. Nor do we know where he was born or where he lived, but it was most likely to have been in the east of modern Iran.

We know a bit more about how he lived his life, because of writings called *gathas* which he composed. He was a member of a priestly family which concerned itself with the worship of the gods who were common to various peoples throughout a vast region from the Middle East to the Indian sub-continent.

At the age of 30, Zoroaster had a vision of an angel-type divine figure, a *yazatah* called Vohu Manah, who led him to Ahura Mazda, one of three creator gods in the religion of the time. As a result of this revelation, Zoroaster began to preach that Ahura Mazda was the sole creator of the universe and source of all good. Yet Zoroaster taught that Ahura Mazda was not all-powerful, and needed human help to beat his opponent Angra Mainyu, the embodiment of evil.

Zoroaster met with many setbacks in his preaching of the new religion, though it gained ground slowly but surely, and his philosophy of good-evil duality influenced the ancient Greeks as they began to craft what became the foundation of western thought.

Many other religions from the Middle East and Asia contained elements of the Zoroastrian philosophy and thinking. Zoroastrianism is still recognised as the first religion founded on reported revelation from God, and, although the rise of Christianity and Islam vastly reduced the number of its adherents, Zoroastrian communities with their distinctly white-clad priestly caste are found in several countries to this day.

·4·

IMMACULATE CONCEPTIONS

Eponymous nouns and verbs, nicknames and honorifics, for human qualities, activities, concepts and types of people.

ACHILLES HEEL

Let's face it – we all have one, a personal weakness that might prove fatal if an opponent could exploit it.

Among the most popular eponyms of them all, and one you might think dates back to antiquity. Not so – the eponymous concept did not appear in literature until the 19th century.

Every schoolchild should know the heel story. In Greek myth, the great warrior Achilles had been made invulnerable by being dipped into the River Styx by his mother, the goddess Thetis. She had to use his heel to hold him in the water, and that one tiny area of his body was where Trojan hero Paris shot him with a poisoned arrow.

It is all myth – Homer's *Iliad* does not refer to Achilles dying at all, and it seems that the various interpreters of

Homer added in the spurious details over the following centuries.

When exactly the Achilles Tendon (see Medical Attributions in chapter 3) was named after the hero is unknown, but a 17th-century Dutch book of anatomy is the first written reference. That usage became more common, but it was Samuel Taylor Coleridge, no less, in referring to Ireland as 'the heel of the British Achilles' in 1810 who gave rise to the eponymous heel we all know so well.

BEAU BRUMMELL

George Bryan Brummell (1778–1840) was the right man in the right place to earn a reputation as the 18th century became the 19th in jolly old Regency England. He was a man of considerably good taste in clothes and, through his friendship with the Prince Regent, he soon became known as England's fashion trendsetter. The best fashion he bequeathed to the nation was his habit of taking a daily bath and shave, and he always kept his teeth clean – this at a time when much of the populace stank to high heaven. He fell out with the Prince, however, famously remarking, 'Who is your fat friend?' when Prince George snubbed him in public. A gambler and a spendthrift who blew his large inheritance in double-quick time, his debts piled up and he eventually had to flee to France where he stayed in relative hardship until his death. Yet such was his reputation for dandiness and elegance that we still call such a person a 'Beau Brummell'.

BENEDICT ARNOLD

Just about the worst thing you can say to an American is to

call them a Benedict Arnold. That's because the original Benedict Arnold (1741–1801) was seen as the greatest traitor to the cause of American independence. Wounded several times in battle, he at first fought for the American colonialists. He had become a general in George Washington's Army and was in command of West Point when his dismay at failing to get the rewards he thought he merited caused him to switch sides and effectively try to sell the fort to the British. The plot was rumbled and Arnold fled, becoming a general in the British Army and being received by King George III as a hero. But the British sense of fair play had been outraged, and Arnold was branded as nothing more than a mercenary, even though he openly campaigned for the citizens of the new United States to return to the British Empire.

British hero, American traitor – whatever you do when you meet Americans, do not try to justify Benedict Arnold's actions.

BENNY

To call someone a 'benny' is downright insulting, whether you do so in the UK or USA, for 'benny' is an example of an eponym that means approximately the same either side of the Atlantic for entirely different reasons.

In America, a benny is specific to the east coast and in Jersey is used to describe an ignorant traveller or incomer from northern cities such as New York. In Maryland, a benny is a dimwit. No one really knows who the original benny was, or why he was so maligned.

The name stuck, however, and is used frequently to this

day, most notably by the 'Benny Go Home' campaign on the Jersey Shore. Apparently, they do not like rude tourists there.

In Britain, the derivation of benny is much more concise. In the 1970s and '80s, the soap opera *Crossroads* featured a character called Benny Hawkins, adroitly played by the actor Paul Henry. Benny was the original 'thick as two short planks' handyman, but he was also a popular chap, as the character stayed in *Crossroads* for 13 years in total.

Benny was much given to displays of bad temper, so 'doing a benny' entered the language. Among children – being the judgemental savages that they are – benny soon became a slang term for anyone of mental slowness, and the term really gained public acceptance during the Falklands War of 1982 when it was revealed that the British soldiers had applied the nickname to the islanders – affectionately, of course.

In *Crossroads*, Benny Hawkins constantly wore a beanie hat, a sort of woollen half-balaclava, long before such an item became fashionable for the umpteenth time. It is possible that, in the public mind, a 'benny' hat became a 'beanie', in which case all those involved in *Crossroads* should accept the role they have played in the history of UK fashion.

BEVIN BOY

From 1943 to 1948, some 48,000 young British men went down the coal mines instead of into the forces. They did so as part of a scheme by Minister of Labour Ernest Bevin (1881–1951) to ensure that coal supplies remained uninterrupted, and thus became Bevin Boys.

BLUEBEARD

Though it's often used as a synonym for a philanderer, strictly speaking a bluebeard is a man who murders his wife. In the case of the original Bluebeard, it was several wives. In the classic tale by Charles Perrault (1628–1703), based on French folklore, he marries a young woman whose curiosity takes her into the room that her new husband had warned her to avoid, whereupon she finds the bodies of all his previous wives. Bluebeard – and yes, he really does have a blue beard in the story – is about to murder her to preserve his secret when her brothers kill him and rescue their sister. The character is supposedly based on French baron Gilles de Rais (1404–40), although his actual predilection was for killing children.

BOBBY

So why is a police officer known as a bobby? That most famous symbol of Britain, the bobby on the beat, is a far cry from the original police forces, of which the most famous were the Bow Street Runners in 18th-century London.

Lawlessness, and particularly gin-sodden drunkenness, was a growing problem throughout the late 18th and 19th centuries, especially in the capital city of the United Kingdom, then the largest metropolis in the world.

Despite hanging, flogging and transportation to the colonies in Australia being the punishment for even the most trivial crimes, villainy actually increased in the early Victorian era, largely because the police forces, such as they were, could not cope.

Along came Sir Robert Peel, a reforming Home Secretary

and later Prime Minister, who was determined to do something to make England a safer place – Scotland always had its separate law system and, in the 19th century, local police services sprang up across that country.

Peel wanted a bigger force, and chose London as the starting point for his bold experiment. At the time, the only crime fighters were the Bow Street Runners, who were attached to the Bow magistrates' court and were few in number. Crucially, the Runners did not patrol the streets. Peel's idea was for a proper 'guard' force, paid to patrol the streets and catch and prosecute criminals. It was not new – there were predecessors in ancient Greece and Rome. What Peel brought to the English justice system, however, was organisation on an unprecedented scale. At first, the Metropolitan force insisted on being called 'policemen', but the nickname 'Peelers' soon stuck. Yet that name did not convey the correct attitude that Peel wanted to encourage – that of policing by consent, still a fundamental tenet of English justice to this day.

'Bobby' soon became the acceptable and accepted nickname for the police, and was even used in Parliament, giving it a veneer of official approval. The bobby on the beat is still the best deterrent to crime, many would argue.

BOWDLERISE

The words 'expletive deleted' became famous when transcripts of the Watergate tapes showed President Richard Nixon and his cronies to be foul-mouthed. Thomas Bowdler (1754–1825) went a lot further, putting a metaphorical red pen through rather a lot of words and sentences in the works of William Shakespeare. Indeed, he did not delete the expletives, he changed them altogether, so that any reference to even slightly questionable material was censored in the edition he called *Family Shakespeare*. For example, Mercutio's line in Romeo and Juliet: 'The bawdy hand of the dial is now upon the prick of noon ...' became 'The hand of the dial is now upon the point of noon ...' while Lady Macbeth's famous line 'Out, damned spot' became 'Out, crimson spot'.

The *Family Shakespeare* sold very well in prim 19th-century England. No wonder that censoring in such a lame manner is known as 'bowdlerising'.

BOYCOTT

One of the most widely used eponyms, the word comes from Captain Charles Boycott (1832–97), a land agent in Ireland who, in 1880, tried to stop the reforming group the Irish Land League from carrying out their campaign against evictions in County Mayo. Boycott, who acted for absentee landlord Lord Erne, was already unpopular because of his strict enforcement of rent payments through evictions, so, when the League organised all the local people to ostracise Boycott, he was soon without servants, shoes for his horse and even his laundry. He wrote a letter to *The Times* and his situation became a cause célèbre, with Orange Order members from Ulster volunteering to help him on his farm, and the British Government sending in police and troops to give them protection. The boycott of Boycott worked – he left Ireland later that year, never to work there again.

BOTCH

Let's kill a legend here, for, uniquely in this book, this word is not an eponym, though far too many people think it is.

A 'botched' job is something to be avoided, and the Tay Railway Bridge in Scotland was definitely worth avoiding in 1879. That was the year the bridge collapsed, due to the design failures of engineer Sir Thomas Bouch. Embarrassing, since he had been knighted just the year before by Queen Victoria in recognition of his work in building the bridge. The generally accepted view had it that 'botch' derived from Bouch, who died ten months after the disaster, but several commentaries of the time show that writers were merely making a play of words on his name, and the fact is that the word 'botch' – meaning 'making a mess' – had been in existence for centuries. You can find it in Shakespeare's *Macbeth*, Act III, 'to leave no rubs nor botches in the work'.

That's the trouble with eponyms – some words which are claimed to be eponymous most definitely are not. 'Botch' turns out to derive from an Old English word meaning 'fix' or 'repair', which became a synonym for the problem which needed repairing.

For a hilarious botch, read William McGonagall's *The Tay Bridge Disaster*, which doesn't even mention poor old Bouch the botcher.

BRAGGADOCIO

All swagger and a complete braggart, the character Braggadocchio made such an impression in Edmund Spenser's epic 16th-century poem *The Faerie Queene* that his name became associated with such behaviour.

BRAIDYS

When James Braidwood became the first director of what is now the London Fire Brigade in 1833, he brought with him the experience of founding – while still in his twenties – the world's first municipal fire service in his native Edinburgh.

Apprenticed to his builder father, Braidwood used the knowledge he gained to devise a scientific method of fighting fires, and his personal bravery was an inspiration to the new brigade – he once calmly removed two smouldering bags of gunpowder from a blazing tenement in Edinburgh's High Street. He invented fire engines and devices for helping people to escape from burning buildings, and made sure his men wore a distinctive uniform.

Moving to London, he transformed the London Fire Engine Establishment and made it a credit to the city. In doing so, he became a very popular figure, credited with the saving of many lives.

When he lost his own life in 1861 while leading the efforts to control the enormous Tooley Street fire, London came to a halt for his funeral, and Queen Victoria recorded her upset at his loss.

By the time of his death, Brigade members were known as Braidys or Jim Braidys after Braidwood, just as Peelers had been the original nickname for the police following their foundation by Sir Robert Peel. Though the term is no longer in general use, a book about the British fire service published in 1943 which featured work by eminent writers such as Stephen Spender was entitled *Jim Braidy, the Story of Britain's Firemen*.

In this politically correct age, firemen and women are all

tagged 'firefighters'. Perhaps we should bring back 'Braidys' in memory of a brave and clever Scot, the father of the British fire service, to whom a statue was finally erected in his home city in 2008.

BUNKUM

It is a word that signifies balderdash and nonsense, usually but not always spoken by politicians, not least because 'bunkum' derives from a political source, the Representative for Buncombe. He was Felix Walker (1753–1838) who represented Buncombe County and other parts of North Carolina in the US Congress. In 1820, he made a fatuous speech full of platitudinous claptrap. He said he had made it for Buncombe, and thus Representative Walker was commemorated in the eponym. Bunk, debunk and hokum are all derived from the same source.

CASANOVA

Giacomo Girolamo Casanova de Seingalt (1725–98) was the world's most famous lover. He was a chronic gambler, a soldier, a spy, a Roman Catholic cleric, a musician, a freemason ... not all in that order, yet all before the age of 35. He was known in the courts of Europe, loved by grand ladies, yet caught a sexually transmitted disease from a lowly prostitute. Imprisoned numerous times for running up hefty debts, he also suffered smallpox and was left with the tell-tale scars of that affliction. Yet, if we believe his beautifully written and often very funny memoirs, he had at least 120 lovers, including some men and boys. His female lovers were significantly in the majority, however, and some estimates put the number of his conquests in four figures. That is why today we call a womaniser a 'Casanova'.

CHURCHILLIAN GESTURE

You could also put the great man's name in front of scowl, oratory, leadership, genius, and equally in front of any word that describes his less positive traits. And yes, his famous 'black dog' of depression was also Churchillian in nature. He remains one of the few politicians to admit to mental illness, although sometimes you could be forgiven for thinking that they are all mad.

Yet there is little doubt that, without Sir Winston Spencer Churchill (1874–1965), this book might well be written in German. In the dark days following the Fall of France, when Hitler's hordes looked set to swamp the whole of Europe, up rose this valiant bulldog of a man, already 65 years old, and, with words crafted in his mind and heart and with the soul of freedom, he and the brave little ships at Dunkirk and the Few of the Battle of Britain turned the tide, or at least stopped the Nazis at the Channel. We British have long realised how much we owe him but, truthfully, we can never owe him enough.

The 'gesture' became his bond with the people. He knew full well what he was doing. The ancient 'V' sign with the two fingers upraised and palm facing backwards was something out of English history, first seen in the 100 Years War with France when deadly archers would wave the 'V' at their opponents in defiance – for they knew that, if captured, archers were liable to have those fingers lopped off.

It was rude, of course, and some people thought it was

a sign for testicles, a British version of the 'evil eye' signal on the Continent. Churchill had thought long and hard about a sign to counteract Hitler's Nazi salute, and came up with 'V' for victory, both fingers raised with the palm turned outwards. He used that 'acceptable' 'V' sign on polite occasions, obviously, but there is ample testament that, during the many visits he paid to troops and civilians alike, Churchill reversed the 'V' and gave 'the fingers' to the enemy.

To this day, Britons usually stick up two fingers to show their contempt (see *Harvey Smith 'V' sign*, chapter 8), while Americans flip one finger. The Churchillian Gesture, like the man himself, is a symbol of Britain. Frankly, it should be treasured, not denigrated.

DOUBTING THOMAS

The apostle Thomas refused to believe that Jesus Christ had risen from the dead unless he could put his finger into the holes caused by the nails, and his hand into the wound caused by the Roman soldier's spear. Jesus appeared to him, showed him the wounds and Doubting Thomas became Thomas the Believer – he is known as both.

DUNCE

John Duns Scotus (1265–1398) was no dunce. Indeed, he was considered to be among the most brilliant men of his time. Born in the town of Duns in the Scottish Borders, he was educated at Oxford and Cambridge before moving to Paris where his scholarship was soon recognised. He became a huge influence on the philosophers and theologians of the time and, as a Franciscan priest, he founded the Scotist school of philosophy which was championed by his order.

The trouble for Scotus is that the followers of other schools of philosophy determined the intellectual path of the church at the time and, as they eventually wrote the church's history, they did their best to ensure that poor John and his adherents were portrayed as intellectually second best – those who followed Scotus were soon known as 'dunces'.

Known during his lifetime as the Subtle Doctor for his bewildering ability to win an argument, Duns Scotus was beatified in 1992 by Pope John Paul II, and is thus called 'Blessed'. He will eventually be canonised, but not as Saint Dunce.

EMINENCE GRISE

There really was a Grey Eminence. The French term means a powerful figure in the background and, for Cardinal Richelieu, the infamous plotter of the *Three Musketeers* fame, that original shadowy personage was a Capuchin friar, Francois Leclerc du Tremblay (1577–1638), whose clerical habit was of the colour then described as *'grise'* (more like our beige).

Richelieu was unflatteringly portrayed by novelist Alexandre Dumas as the chief schemer of France who had King Louis XIII in his pocket. In fact, he was a loyal supporter of the King who used his undoubted talents for skulduggery to consolidate the monarch and establish France as a modern state, while also founding the Académie Française.

In this work, he was assisted by Leclerc, also known as

Père Joseph, an aristocrat who renounced worldly riches and who became Richelieu's most trusted adviser and confidant, as adept at political intrigue as his master. Just as Cardinal Duc de Richelieu was known as the Red Eminence, so Père Joseph became the Eminence Grise. Aldous Huxley, author of *Brave New World*, wrote a biography of Leclerc entitled *The Grey Eminence* which was published in 1941.

EPICURE

There are usually two meanings for this word. One is similar to 'gourmet', namely a person of good taste in food and drink, while the other is akin to 'gourmand', describing a person who loves sensuous living, especially lots of rich food. The word derives from the name of Epicurus (341–270BC), a philosopher who preached the pursuit of happiness as the goal of life in his school in Athens known as The Garden.

FANNY ADAMS

When we talk of Fanny Adams, Sweet Fanny Adams or Sweet FA, we all know what we are talking about – nothing at all. Sweet Fanny Adams is the eponym used mainly in Britain to describe nothingness or the state of being rewarded with zero. Sweet FA is also a euphemism for 'sweet f*** all', which describes 'nothing whatsoever'.

It is highly likely that only a very few people know who the eponymous Fanny Adams was, or else they would refrain from using the term out of respect for a young murder victim.

For Fanny Adams was a real little girl, just eight years old when she was picked out in random fashion and murdered most horribly by Frederick Baker, a solicitor's clerk and supposed gentleman, at Alton in Hampshire in 1867.

Fanny and two little friends were out playing when Baker approached them and offered the other girls money for sweets but then insisted on Fanny going with him. She took a halfpenny and it sealed her fate, as Baker dragged her into a field of hops away from the other girls who, thinking him respectable, carried on playing. As they did so, Baker brutally murdered Fanny, crushing her skull, decapitating her and then butchering her body so savagely that it took several days to find all her scattered limbs and organs – her eyes were found in a nearby river.

Baker protested his innocence, but his only real defence was insanity – there was a streak of it in the family. The jury gave that short shrift and took 15 minutes to find him guilty. He was hanged in front of a crowd of 5,000 on Christmas Eve 1867, in Worcester. Baker admitted to the crime in a last letter to Fanny's parents, asking for their forgiveness.

The name of the Alton Murderer became notorious across Victorian Britain, and the entirely gruesome way in which Fanny met her end became widely known.

With typically dark, military humour, not long afterwards, when the Royal Navy began to dispense half-empty rations of less than wholesome mutton made of a range of cheap and insubstantial cuts, the ratings likened the contents to Sweet Fanny Adams, and the words spread to other branches of the service and then into general usage. There is ample proof of the derivation – in some parts of the Navy, mess tins and cooking pots are still called 'fannys' or 'fannies'.

Next time you get sweet FA for your efforts, console

yourself that you are still better off than poor Fanny Adams, the sweet child whose name came to signify nothing.

FOXTROT

Named after American dancer and comedian Harry Fox (1882–1959) who first devised the steps just before the outbreak of the First World War. It's just as well that Harry used his stage name for the dance, otherwise millions of people would have danced the Carringford-trot, his real name being Arthur Carringford.

GAIA THEORY

Environmentalist James Lovelock called his theory – that the Earth is a complex, living organism which is self-regulating – after the Greek goddess of the planet, a figure somewhat like Mother Nature. Lovelock has always stated that the name was suggested by his friend and neighbour William Golding, author of *Lord of the Flies*.

HOBSON'S CHOICE

It is often thought that Hobson's choice means there is no choice at all, but that is not the original meaning. Thomas Hobson (1544–1631) was the owner of large horse stables near Cambridge University who made a good living out of renting his horses to students and local citizens. To preserve their health and usefulness, Hobson worked out a strict rotation policy for his animals, telling his clients that they had to take the horse in the stall nearest the stable door, i.e. the next one up. Either that, or they could walk rather than ride. So Hobson's choice is really this – you can choose what you are offered, or choose to walk away. But you still have a choice; 'my way or the highway', as modern Hobsons would put it.

All references (and there are many) to the eponym being 'Hobbesian Choice' are wrong. Hobbesian refers to the works and thought of the English philosopher Thomas Hobbes (1588–1679), he who opined that the life of humans without a State or law and order is 'solitary, poor, nasty, brutish and short'. Given the option, most of us wouldn't want a Hobbesian choice.

HOOKER

It was long thought that this nickname for a prostitute derived from General Joseph Hooker (1814–79), the famous 'Fighting Joe' of the Union Army in the American Civil War. Though he suffered a few setbacks, including heavy defeat by Robert E Lee's Confederate Army in the Battle of Chancellorsville, Hooker was a competent general who enjoyed a reputation for devotion to the welfare of his soldiers. This extended to allowing female camp followers, many of whom were prostitutes. In time, they became known as Hooker's Brigade or Hooker's Division, and it was said that the General 'took some comfort there', in Paul Simon's memorable phrase in the song 'The Boxer'.

Sadly for the legend, the word 'hooker' was already in existence some years before the war, deriving from the Corlear's Hook area of Manhattan island where prostitutes plied their trade openly. Still, Hooker's fame and his reputation as a hard-fighting, hard-playing man probably helped to popularise the term.

HOOLIGANISM

Another highly disputed eponym, about which even the most scholarly of dictionaries disagree. The word certainly derives from the not uncommon Irish surname O'Houlihan or Houlihan (c.f. Margaret 'Hot Lips' Houlihan in *M*A*S*H*), but whether that transformed into hooligan by way of a music hall song, or the activities of a rowdy family in Ireland in the 19th century, or through an infamous streetfighter in London in the late Victorian era is something of a moot point.

Recent research indicates that the first use of the word was in newspaper accounts of trials in 1890 involving young criminals in the south Lambeth area of London. They were described in press accounts of trials as 'the Hooligan Boys', as they had Irish leaders, at least one of whom was a Houlihan. The Irish form of that name, which is presumably what was on the charge sheets, is written as 'O hUallacháin' – you can see for yourself that it might well be written or said in English as 'hooligan'. The eponym caught on. Sadly, so did hooliganism.

JEKYLL AND HYDE

If we say someone is a Jekyll and Hyde character, we usually mean they are quick to change from nice to nasty, or vice versa. The eponym comes from *The Strange Case of Dr Jekyll and Mr Hyde* by Robert Louis Stevenson (1850–94), the novelist who was a bit of a dual personality himself, at least in his younger days. Outwardly respectable, the son of the great Stevenson family of Scottish engineers and lighthouse builders was a law student by day but frequented

Edinburgh's many fine pubs by night – they are still pretty good – as well as brothels and private clubs dedicated to hellraising. When it came to finding inspiration for Jekyll and Hyde, Stevenson had only to look in the mirror.

JEZEBEL

In our modern understanding, a jezebel is a dominant woman who is usually prepared to use her sexuality to get her way. The original Jezebel can be found in the two Books of Kings in the Old Testament, and she really wasn't a very nice girl at all, according to the people who wrote the Bible. But they were biased. A princess of Phoenicia, she married King Ahab of the Israelites, converted him to the worship of Baal and other Phoenician gods, and slaughtered the prophets who disagreed with her. With some amazing firepower, the prophet Elijah proved that his one true God, Yahweh, was more powerful than Baal and his cohorts, and Jezebel was furious.

After King Ahab's death, she carried on her 'countless harlotries and sorceries', as it states in the Bible, until Jehu killed her son King Joram in a palace coup and then came after her. Undaunted, Jezebel put on her face paint and her best outfit and sat at the upstairs window taunting Jehu, who ordered her own eunuchs to throw down the former queen. With a fine disregard for loyalty and an eye to their own survival, the eunuchs obliged Jehu, and Jezebel was dashed to the ground and trampled to bloody bits under the feet of Jehu's cavalry horses. Nice people, those ancient Israelites.

For some modern feminists, Jezebel is seen as a heroine, a strong woman who was the real power in the kingdom, so calling a female a jezebel may no longer be an insult. Just don't try it in the office.

JOHN HANCOCK

When he came to sign the Declaration of Independence, John Hancock (1736–93) did not mess about. A rich and hugely influential merchant from Massachusetts – it was said he financed the American Revolution – the British accused him of smuggling, but the charges did not stick. He became the President of the Continental Congress which declared independence in 1776. His bold signature is still seen as the most florid on the document and, in time, Americans came to call any signature a 'John Hancock', proving that, like their British cousins, they will create an eponym out of respect.

JONAH

We call a person or thing that brings bad luck a 'jonah', because the Prophet Jonah in the Old Testament survived a run of bad luck. Yet, when you consider what happened to him, you might easily conclude that Jonah experienced more good luck than bad. Admittedly, it was pretty bad luck to be swallowed whole by a whale, but he survived, didn't he?

JUDAS

A Judas is a traitor, most correctly used of a friend or colleague who betrays you. The four main gospels all agree that the apostle Judas Iscariot (the derivation of his surname is uncertain) betrayed Jesus to the Jewish authorities and the Romans. The details are inconsistent about how exactly he betrayed Jesus, or how he was overcome by shame and hanged himself, but they all agree that Judas was the instigator of the arrest that led to Jesus's crucifixion.

Intriguingly, a supposed 'Gospel according to Judas' surfaced in the 1970s, in which it was claimed that Jesus knew all about Judas's plan to betray him and indeed approved of it so that the ancient prophecies about the Messiah could be fulfilled.

JUGGERNAUT

The proverbial irresistible force, the name has been used for massive trucks and tanks, large ships and at least two movies featuring murderers who seemingly can't be stopped.

Yet the original Juggernaut was nothing more than an image of the Hindu god Vishnu, one of whose titles is 'Jagganath', meaning Lord of the World. It was a very large image, carried on huge carts from the temple in Puri, India, and, according to scurrilous European reports, people would throw themselves in front of the cart to gain martyrdom. Not actually true, as the real problem was the sheer size of the Jagganath in close proximity to excited crowds. But it made for good gossip in the days of the Raj, and Jagganath was soon translated to 'Juggernaut', being applied to vehicles that just kept growing.

The journey from Hindu god to 40-tonne truck is another example of how eponyms develop, and it's certainly one of the more bizarre derivations.

LYNCHING

One of those hotly disputed eponyms, the word for a mob's

revenge killing of a guilty or innocent person is usually said to come from Charles Lynch (1736–96), an American patriot from Virginia who became a militia colonel in the battle against the British in the War of Independence. A former Quaker, Lynch became a justice of the peace and used the office to begin what he himself called 'Lynch Law', in which he and his colleagues terrorised those residents of Virginia who sided with the British.

Trials were a mere irritation to Lynch as he handed out sentences ranging from forced conscription to whipping. He never actually 'lynched' anyone – i.e. hanged them from a tree – but that was soon a common occurrence in the USA, as the deep south in particular saw lynch mobs, often organised by the Ku Klux Klan, hang many more black people than white without resorting to the justice system.

Other Lynches in America and Ireland have been claimed as the original 'lynch', but Charles has by far the best provenance.

MALAPROPISM

A malapropism is an accidental or deliberate witticism created by using a wrong word, especially one that sounds or looks like the word that was originally intended to be used.

The best malapropisms are always the accidental ones – but the originator of the term deliberately coined malapropisms for intentional comic effect. Richard Brinsley Sheridan created the character Mrs Malaprop in his 1775 play *The Rivals*, productions of which take place to this day. No wonder, as the play is very funny with Mrs Malaprop providing some of the most hilarious moments with her mangling of the language.

Among her gaffes is 'he is the very pineapple [pinnacle] of politeness' and 'he's as headstrong as an allegory [alligator] on the banks of the Nile'.

Malapropisms were not new in 1775. Shakespeare abounds with them, particularly Dogberry in *Much Ado about Nothing*. They have long been a staple of comedy in books, films and television shows – 'What are you incinerating [insinuating]?' as Harold Steptoe said, or possibly the funniest of them all from the Marx Brothers' film *A Night at the Opera*: 'You can't fool me, there ain't no sanity clause [Santa Claus]!'

President George W Bush frequently 'mis-spoke' as he put it – 'the illiteracy of our children are [is] appalling …' – but these Bushisms were not true malapropisms, just garbled speech, though he did once say he had been 'pillared [pilloried] by the press'.

My own grandmother, Minnie Caulfield, was famous in our family for accidentally spouting them. She spoke of her hands being 'dumb [numb] with cold' and described the apes of Gibraltar as 'those hairy bassoons [baboons]', though she never said 'last will and testicle [testament]' – that was me as a schoolboy.

MARTINET

Usually employed to describe a strict disciplinarian, the eponym is apposite, as it derives from General Jean Martinet, drillmaster in the armies of King Louis XIV in 17th-century France. He made the French Army a formidable fighting force, but angered his own troops with his unrelenting severity. The common view is that, having provoked them once too often, he was killed by his own soldiers under cover of enemy fire at the Siege of Duisburg in 1672.

MASOCHISM

Regularly paired with sadism, masochism is a sexual fetish in which gratification is derived from pain or humiliation. It is named after Leopold von Sacher-Masoch (1836–95), an Austrian novelist who, like the Marquis de Sade, wrote about his sexual fantasies and experiences, in his case the true story of how he agreed to act as the slave of his mistress, Baroness Fanny Pistor, for six months, as long as she wore furs while humiliating him. He wrote a thinly disguised account of their activities in his novella *Venus in Furs*.

Like de Sade, he went quite mad.

MAVERICK

There are, no doubt, some people who think we get the word 'maverick' from the American television Western series of that name which made a star of the much underrated James Garner. They are not completely wrong, because the word derives from a heroic figure of the Old West, Samuel Augustus Maverick, who was not a gambler but a lawyer who kept some cattle on the side.

Confusingly, there is another prominent Samuel Maverick in American history, but he was a 17th-century English colonist in Massachusetts and has no connection to the word.

Born in 1803 in South Carolina, Sam Maverick moved to Texas with his young wife Mary. We know a great deal about them, principally because Sam wrote a journal, Mary kept a diary and his son George also wrote about him, all of these accounts being later published.

His father's success in business meant that Sam Maverick could buy a lot of land in Texas, which was then part of Mexico. He then became involved in the revolution which led to the Texan Declaration of Independence, and was imprisoned by the Mexicans for his stance.

Having acquired 400 head of cattle in payment for a debt, Maverick seems genuinely not to have cared about what happened to his animals, which were left to roam about the area. Unbranded cattle in Texas thus became known as 'mavericks' and the word soon spread, coming to mean a person who refused to conform and which is now used in the sense of wild and unpredictable.

Again, he is one of the people whose name became an eponym during his life because 'maverick' was first written in its accepted sense in 1867, three years before the real Maverick died in San Antonio. Maverick County in Texas is also named after him.

MENTOR

This word signifying a teacher-figure or adviser derives from the Greek mythological figure of Mentor, the friend of Odysseus who takes charge of his son Telemachus when Odysseus goes off to fight in the Trojan War and then gets lost for a decade.

METHUSELAH

Whenever reference is being made to someone in extreme old

age – or a joke is being made about someone who just acts old – sooner or later a person will be called a 'Methuselah'. The name comes from the Bible, from the Book of Genesis, where Methuselah is referred to as the grandfather of Noah. He apparently lived to the age of 969, and tradition has it that the Great Flood started seven days after his death, as God delayed the rain to allow for the official period of mourning. Whether legend or myth, Methuselah's great longevity still has a powerful hold on modern imagination – in 2010, when scientists discovered that a particular gene could hold the reason why some people live to beyond 100 and most of us do not, it was immediately christened the 'Methuselah' gene.

Methuselah is also a bottle size, equivalent to eight times the standard wine bottle. You would need to live as long as Methuselah to consume all that, surely.

MICAWBER

To call someone a Micawber, or describe them as Micawberish, is not the worst insult you can fling. After all, the character of Wilkins Micawber in Charles Dickens' novel *David Copperfield* is quite lovable in his own way. Micawber was poor, but thought that better times were always around the corner. Micawber? We are all him, are we not?

MIDAS TOUCH

King Midas was the Sultan of Brunei or the Bill Gates of his day, the wealthiest man alive. Though there may well have been a king named Midas somewhere in the Greek lands in the early part of the 1st millennium BC, his name is handed down to us from the Greek myths, most famously for the fable in which he asks the gods for the power to turn anything he touches to gold, only to find he can't eat. Other versions have Midas becoming a follower of the god Pan, and falling out with Apollo, who turns his ears into those of a donkey. Either way, the very rich Midas ended up a very unhappy king, which is exactly what those moral Greek mythologists wanted us to think.

MNEMONICS

A word or phrase to aid memory, mnemonics are linked to Mnemosyne, the Greek goddess of memory. The original Greek word '*mnemon*' had a meaning of remembrance, and whether the word or goddess arrived first is lost in antiquity.

NEMESIS

The goddess of revenge in Greek mythology, she is usually depicted with wings, almost as an angel of retribution.

ODYSSEY

Somewhat strangely, in those bygone days when Classics were still taught at most British schools, the hero of Homer's *Odyssey* was known as Ulysses to most people. That is largely because Latin was considerably more popular than Greek, and Ulysses is the Latin form of Odysseus. Yet, when we speak or write of a long journey or a complicated trip, we call it an odyssey. That's English for you.

According to Homer, Odysseus was the King of Ithaca who went off to fight Troy with the rest of the Greek Army, but somehow got sidetracked on the way home and took ten years to be reunited with his beloved and faithful wife

Penelope, having survived encounters with monsters and seductively voiced women – the eponymous Sirens – on the way. No wonder we call a tough journey an odyssey.

PANDER

To pander to someone usually means to satisfy their demands, but, in its original sense, to pander meant to cater for someone's sexual desires, and pander is still sometimes used as another word for pimp. It comes from Pandarus, who, in the original poetic tales by Giovanni Boccaccio and Geoffrey Chaucer, is the go-between who fixes it for Troilus and Cressida – as they were later called by Shakespeare – to become lovers.

PAPARAZZI

The great Italian director Federico Fellini settled on the name Paparazzo for a news photographer, a character in his film *La Dolce Vita*, though whether he got the name from a childhood acquaintance or from a character in a travel book is not known.

'Paparazzi' is the plural form of the name in Italian.

PAUL JONES (DANCE)

Though the reason why is obscure, this dance is named after John Paul Jones (1747–92), the Scots-born sea captain credited with being the founding father of the American Navy.

During the American War of Independence, Jones famously led the British Navy a merry dance. It is not often recalled by Americans that, having laid the foundations of their Navy, Jones then went off and helped another country to get their Navy up and running – Russia.

PILATES

Joseph Pilates (1883–1967) devised the system of physical fitness routines which bear his name. Born in Germany, he was a sickly child who trained hard from his early days to build up his strength. He emigrated to England and was interned along with other German citizens in a camp on the Isle of Man. It was there while working as a hospital orderly that he added the body movements which will be familiar to any Pilates student and, after re-emigrating to New York in the 1920s, he began to teach his methods, with classes now spread around the world.

PONZI SCHEME

The proof that suckers are born every minute is the continuing emergence of Ponzi Schemes. Charles Ponzi (1882–1949) was an Italian fraudster who invented the eponymous scheme in which people invest in a money-making scam that promises a high rate of return – in his case, a swindle involving international mail reply coupons – and are paid their profits from later investors until the rate of new investment dries up and can't meet the earlier commitments.

Ponzi was exposed by the *Boston Post* newspaper and he went to prison for mail fraud. Undaunted, he tried similar schemes elsewhere in the USA, but eventually was deported to Italy and ended his days in poverty in Brazil.

The best known of recent Ponzi Schemes was operated by Bernard Madoff, a New York businessman, whose scam involved the sum of $65 billion! He is now serving 150 years in jail and has been ordered to pay back $18 billion to those he conned.

QUISLING

Seldom can one man have seen his reputation so comprehensively trashed both during and after his life. But then Vidkun Quisling (1887–1945) deserves to have his name used to describe traitorous co-operation with an enemy, for that is exactly what he did in Norway during the Second World War.

Born a clergyman's son in 1887, he became the most brilliant student the Norwegian Military College had ever seen, and he turned himself into Norway's main expert on Russia, a country which fascinated him. After leaving the Army, he entered diplomatic service and there encountered the Nazis in Germany. He was influenced to form and lead the quasi-fascist National Unity party which did not amount to much until Germany occupied Norway. Quisling had assisted the invasion, and was rewarded with being made head of the puppet government. He ruled the country with terror and committed Norway to various Nazi ideals such as the persecution of Jews, yet he was Hitler's least favourite poodle, even the Führer realising that Quisling was over the top in his obsequiousness.

When Germany surrendered, the re-formed Norwegian Government put Quisling on trial and he was executed for crimes such as murder and conspiring with the Nazi invaders. He was executed by firing squad, a fate that all such quislings should meet.

RACHMANISM

Peter Rachman (1919–62) was a landlord in London who exploited vulnerable tenants to make a fortune. While his henchmen bullied and threatened his mostly immigrant tenants – he was an immigrant himself, having been born in what was then Poland – he drove a Rolls-Royce, charmed countless women into bed and, despite being married, had two rather famous mistresses, Christine Keeler and Mandy Rice-Davies, the girls who were later at the centre of the infamous Profumo Affair.

Rachman may have been a charmer, but his business methods were very unpleasant indeed, and his villainy deserves to be recalled by a hateful word.

RAMBO

When someone is described as a Rambo or Rambo type, we conjure up an image of a psychotic on the rampage, such as Raoul Moat who killed one man and put the fear of God into much of north-east England in 2010.

Sylvester Stallone's portrayal in three films of John Rambo, a former Vietnam War Special Forces veteran turned one-man killing machine, made the name synonymous with vengeful outrage by a steroid-enhanced muscle man.

Yet, in the original novel, *First Blood*, by David Morrell, John Rambo is a highly intelligent and sympathetic character, a man much more sinned against than sinning who only responds to violence – albeit with 'extreme prejudice', as the CIA might say – after provocation. Still, the movies nearly always set the agenda these days, so Stallone's characterisation is why we use 'Rambo' to describe such people.

In the book, it should be said, Rambo dies at the end, but the film-makers couldn't risk missing out on a sequel, could they?

RITZ

When Fred Astaire and Ginger Rogers danced to the song 'Putting on the Ritz', they were merely confirming on screen what was already accepted in popular culture – that the glitziest and smartest place around was the Ritz Hotel. It's why we also use the word 'ritzy' as the adjective to describe classy and upmarket.

It will probably upset Londoners, but the original Ritz Hotel was in Paris, opened in 1898 by César Ritz (1858–1919), the Swiss-born hotelier who had previously managed the Savoy in London where his friend, the chef Auguste Escoffier, had transformed the menu.

Horror of horrors, the Paris Ritz, and therefore the Ritz chain, was founded in somewhat shady circumstances. Ritzy people do not like to be reminded that old César was sacked from the Savoy after a king's ransom in booze went missing from the cellars. A year later and Ritz was opening France's best hotel. Coincidence?

ROMEO

In Shakespeare's *Romeo and Juliet*, the story is one of doomed love, with the male half of the duet being young, impulsive and definitely dead by the end. In modern usage, a romeo is simply a philanderer, doomed or otherwise.

By the way, when Juliet says, 'Wherefore art thou Romeo?' she is not referring to his position below the balcony, but is asking, 'Why are you called Romeo?' as 'wherefore' is an old English word meaning 'why'. And while you may have known that, wherefore shouldn't I mention it to those who didn't?

SADISM

The Marquis de Sade (1740–1814) was not the only French nobleman of his time to have a curious sex life. He was one of very few to write about it, however, thus winning undying fame, or infamy if you prefer, for the practice of inflicting pain or punishment for sexual gratification.

His given name was Donatien Alphonse François, and his family were of ancient French nobility. He had a normal childhood, although education by the Jesuits can play havoc with the mind – as the author can personally testify!

De Sade entered the Army and rose to become a colonel in the dragoons of the French King's Army during the Seven Years War. He also married Renée-Pélagie de Montreuil and had three children by her, despite actually loving her sister. So far, so good – then de Sade went seriously off the rails after his father died in 1767.

He had already been in trouble for ill-treating prostitutes, but nobody really bothered about that in those pre-Revolutionary days. When he imprisoned a woman who may not have been a prostitute in his castle in Provence and sexually abused her, de Sade got into serious trouble, but that was nothing to the events of 1772 when he was accused of having sex with his manservant – it was apparently the indignity of him consorting with the lower classes that really upset the authorities.

Sentenced to death for the capital offence of sodomy, he and his servant ran away to Italy. He returned when the hue and cry had died down, and he and his wife and her sister formed a bizarre ménage à trois, before de Sade began even more extreme forms of sexual behaviour and writing about them, turning some experiences into scenes in his novels *Justine* and *The 120 Days of Sodom*.

All Europe being scandalised by his work, de Sade was declared insane and put in the Bastille, and his wife eventually divorced him. Growing fat and indeed quite mad, he was banned from writing both his philosophical works and his accounts of depravity. He remains a figure of fascination for many people to this day.

SAPPHISM

Another word for lesbianism, derived from the poetess Sappho of Lesbos. We know little for certain about her as she lived from near the end of the 7th century BC to about 570BC and not much of her work has survived. In her time, though, she was famed as one of the greatest of Greek poets, a particular distinction given her gender and the diminished status of women in Greek society.

The problem of the association between Sappho and indeed the island of Lesbos and lesbianism is that it is all pure conjecture. Despite the erotic nature of her poetry about women, nobody in antiquity thought Sappho was a lesbian and they probably wouldn't have cared anyway, as they were rather more sanguine about homosexuality in those days. References to Sapphism in conjunction with lesbianism turn out to be a pretty modern invention, no older than the 19th century when Queen Victoria famously refused to believe such a thing existed.

SCROOGE

A miserly soul is known as a Scrooge after the misanthropic character of Ebenezer Scrooge in Charles Dickens' novel *A Christmas Carol*. Dickens took the name from a Mr Ebenezer Scroggie, a merchant whose gravestone he noticed in the burial yard of Canongate in Edinburgh. The gravestone was lost when Canongate Kirkyard was redeveloped in the 1930s. As it turned out, Mr Scroggie was actually a happy and generous soul, much given to partying, which is how Scrooge turns out in the book.

SHERLOCK

'No s**t, Sherlock.' His name has passed into common usage to signify someone of superior intellect, or as almost a generic term for detectives. Sherlock Holmes first saw the light of day in *A Study in Scarlet* by Sir Arthur Conan Doyle (1859–1930), a story published in 1887, and went on to feature in 4 novels and 56 stories, from which hundreds of films and television adaptations have followed. A qualified medical doctor, Conan Doyle based elements of Holmes on Dr Joseph Bell and Sir Henry Littlejohn, having encountered both men at Edinburgh University. He named the detective after Oliver Wendell Holmes, the 'Great Dissenter' of the American legal system, and chose the name Sherlock from a cricketer he knew, having first of all used 'Sherrinford'. Dr Watson was named after a doctor friend of Conan Doyle, only with the names 'John H' switched for 'James'.

Conan Doyle was aware in his lifetime that Sherlock Holmes was so famous that he swamped all his other work and even the fame of the writer himself. It remains the case long after his death – there is one statue of Conan Doyle which stands in Crowborough where he lived for 23 years, while four statues of Holmes have been erected (albeit to honour Conan Doyle, too) in London, Edinburgh, Karuizawa in Japan and Meiringen in Switzerland near the Reichenbach Falls where the detective had his famous fight with Professor Moriarty.

Holmes' fans, by the way, are known as 'Sherlockians'. As another 'by the way', it should be noted that, in Conan Doyle's works, Holmes never once said, 'Elementary, my dear Watson.'

SPOONERISM

Poor William Archibald Spooner (1844–1930). The Reverend gentleman devoted almost his entire life to New College, Oxford, latterly becoming its Dean and then Warden until his retirement in 1924. And what is he remembered for? A slip of the tongue in which the initial letters or syllables of two words were transposed to accidental comic effect.

Spooner himself claimed he only ever did it once, referring to a hymn in 1879 as 'Kinkering Congs Their Titles Take', but that was enough for his colleagues and students to invent a whole list of 'spoonerisms'. Though at first he detested his reputation for gaffes, Reverend Spooner may even have joined in the game, as he is acknowledged to have minted a few of the better-known ones himself – 'the weight of rages will press hard upon the employer' is even in the *Oxford Dictionary of Quotations* against his name.

Accidental or wittily deliberate, actually spoken by him or mischievously credited to him, some of the clergyman's spoonerisms are now legendary – 'let us raise our glass to the queer old dean' and 'we'll have the hags flung out' and 'you have hissed all my mystery lectures' are just three he is supposed to have uttered.

Many more deliberate spoonerisms and variations on the theme have followed from other people. That witty lady Dorothy Parker once said, 'I'd rather have a bottle in front of me than a frontal lobotomy,' and comedian Ronnie Barker loved to use them – he once did a sketch entirely consisting of spoonerisms, playing Rev Spooner and including some of Spooner's own. See for yourself on YouTube.

SVENGALI

A person who holds undue influence over others is said to be a 'svengali'. The name comes from a character in the novel *Trilby* by George du Maurier which was published in 1894. George du Maurier, grandfather of novelist Dame Daphne du Maurier, was a cartoonist for *Punch* magazine whose work was highly prized, and he also illustrated major novels of the Victorian era. Later in his career, he wrote three novels, of which *Trilby* was by far the biggest seller, second only at the time to *Dracula* by Bram Stoker.

In the book, illustrated by du Maurier himself, Trilby O'Ferrall, an artist's model, falls under the spell of musician and hypnotist Svengali who makes her into a great singer as long as she is under his spell. Svengali dies suddenly before a performance and Trilby is exposed as tone deaf.

Viewed from a modern-day standpoint, the novel is frankly dreadful, though the scene where Trilby dies after finally singing one last song is quite affecting – you can read it online in free e-book format. Clearly inspiring Gaston Leroux's novel *The Phantom of the Opera*, *Trilby* was made into a massively successful play and the inevitable film some years later was entitled *Svengali*. The character of Svengali became fixed in public culture and the name has been used ever since.

Curiously, the novel also gave another word to English – the use of 'altogether' to mean nude, as Trilby poses naked for artists and du Maurier had to find a polite shorthand for 'without clothes'.

TANTALISE

This alluring word for teasing and titillating comes from Tantalus, a figure from Greek mythology who, tantalisingly, may have been based on a real person. Supposedly the King of Anatolia or Phrygia (in modern-day Turkey), Tantalus departed history and entered mythology by angering the gods – he served them a feast made from the chopped-up body of his own son. He may also have stolen the food and drink of the gods, ambrosia and nectar, and given them to mortals.

Whatever he did, the gods of Olympus were not pleased and, as a result, he was banished to the Underworld and condemned to stand in a lake for ever. Every time he reached up to grab fruit from an overhanging tree, the branch withdrew, and every time he bent to drink from the lake, the water shrank away from him, so that he spent eternity just out of reach of sustenance.

TAYLORISM

The founding father of scientific management, Frederick Winslow Taylor (1856–1915), was originally an engineer. He devised methods that allowed factories to stay in continuous production, and stressed that good management was about seeking improvements in every process. His ideas on efficiency in the workplace influenced generations of both capitalists and socialists – Lenin and Stalin were particular admirers.

UNCLE SAM

It's another hotly disputed term, with historians and etymologists arguing the case that it is definitely, or absolutely not, eponymous.

The expression which is commonly used to mean the American Government, and sometimes the United States in its entirety, certainly derives from the initials 'US' but possibly also from a real person. Sam Wilson was an American of Scottish parentage who was a meat packer in Troy, New York, at the outbreak of the 1812 war between the USA and Britain. He supplied the beef in barrels marked 'US', and soldiers allegedly began to use the expression 'Uncle Sam' in gratitude to Wilson – rather than the Government – for keeping them fed.

The problem with this story is that only a few newspapers mentioned the Uncle Sam connection when

Wilson died in 1854, but then newspaper people have notoriously short memories. The use of Uncle Sam to mean the Government was even adopted by that Government itself, as the name was used in recruiting posters. Congress had no doubts in 1961 – it passed a resolution saluting Sam Wilson as 'the progenitor of America's national symbol of Uncle Sam'.

VAN DYCK BEARD

A jutting hirsute presence on the male chin with the facial hair removed from the cheeks between sideburns and chin, the Van Dyck beard is perhaps not as fashionable as it once was. Flemish artist Anthony van Dyck (1599–1641) wore one himself and from his self-portrait we know that to be a proper Van Dyck; a beard must be a goatee with a moustache, whether or not the two are connected. His most famous client was King Charles I of Great Britain, who also wore a Van Dyck. Yet, unusually for eponyms, it is the artist and not the aristocrat who is remembered.

ZAPATA MOUSTACHE

The Mexican revolutionary, Emiliano Zapata Salazar (1879–1919), who was dismissed as a bandit by his opponents but is revered as a nation founder by ordinary Mexicans, always wore a magnificent moustache, though technically it was not a Zapata. A true Zapata, as defined by barbers over many years, should 'droop' down from both sides of the lips towards the chin. Yet pictures of Zapata show him wearing a full moustache which protruded to the sides and not down his face.

According to his biographers, Zapata was proud of his 'tache, and kept it constantly waxed so that it did not droop except in very hot or very wet weather. So, more Poirot than Zapata.

·5·

LAYING DOWN
THE LAW

Eponymous laws, their originators and their derivations.

ASIMOV'S LAWS

The famous Three Laws of Robotics were first defined by
the scientist and author Isaac Asimov (1920–92), the Russian-
born American citizen who became one of the greatest names
in science-fiction. Asimov, who coined the word 'robotics'
which is now a standard term in English, devised the Three
Laws almost as a work in progress in his early stories.
Eventually, he defined them in his short story *Runaround*,
published in 1942:

1. *A robot may not injure a human being or, through
   inaction, allow a human being to come to harm.*
2. *A robot must obey any orders given to it by human
   beings, except where such orders would conflict with
   the First Law.*
3. *A robot must protect its own existence as long as*

such protection does not conflict with the First or Second Law.

The Three Laws were to be a huge factor in Asimov's career, the author basing many plots on how they could be interpreted or disregarded. The key Asimov assertion that all 'thinking' robots would have the Three Laws built into their 'positronic' brains is now accepted as likely when science does eventually produce robots with that level of intelligence.

Asimov wrote hundreds of novels and short stories, including the best-selling and massively influential *Foundation* series, as well as textbooks on science – he was a professor of biochemistry – and even acted as a technical adviser on a *Star Trek* film as he was friendly with producer Gene Roddenberry. Judging by the fact that they are still quoted and debated by writers and scientists alike nearly 70 years later, it seems that Asimov's Three Laws of Robotics will be his greatest legacy.

CLARKE'S THREE LAWS OF PREDICTION

As one of the other great science-fiction writers of the latter half of the 20th century, British writer and scientist Arthur C Clarke (1917–2008) was not going to let Isaac Asimov be the only author with three eponymous laws. Though it took him many years, Clarke finally formulated his own trio of laws which are about prediction, and show that he had a sense of humour:

1. *When a distinguished but elderly scientist states that something is possible, he is almost certainly right;*

when he states that something is impossible, he is probably wrong.

2. *The only way of discovering the limits of the possible is to venture a little way past them into the impossible.*

3. *Any sufficiently advanced technology is indistinguishable from magic.*

Unlike Asimov, Clarke did not make his Three Laws an integral part of his work, but he returned to the subject with glee in 1999, adding a Fourth Law: '*For every expert there is an equal and opposite expert.*'

Clarke was also a genius at prediction, proving that his Second Law worked by taking imaginative leaps towards what seemed impossible. Many years before they became reality, he predicted satellite communication technology, mobile phones, surveys to find rogue asteroids (now called Near-Earth Objects), cryogenics and even the Millennium Bug.

Now that sort of foresight is surely the stuff of alchemy.

DILBERT PRINCIPLE
(*See* **Peter Principle** *below*)

One of the funniest long-running cartoon strips with a huge devoted following, Dilbert is the work of Scott Adams (b. 1957) who turns his cynical eye on everything from politics to corporate 'speak' and human resources.

Adams waded into the latter field in response to the development of the Peter Principle, which states that competent employees get promoted to the level where they become incompetent. In turn, Adams devised his own satirical view. Basically, the Dilbert Principle holds that incompetent employees get promoted to the level where they can do least damage, i.e. by becoming managers.

The Dilbert Principle struck a chord – when Adams made a book out of it with cartoons and essays in *A Cubicle's-Eye View of Bosses, Meetings, Management Fads and Other Workplace Afflictions*, his book *The Dilbert Principle* shot to the top of best-seller lists and indeed stayed on the *New York Times'* list for 43 weeks.

DOLLO'S LAW OF IRREVERSIBILITY

This has been a controversial Law ever since it was pronounced by the Belgian palaeontologist Louis Dollo in 1893. Dollo stated that evolution was irreversible, putting it like this: '*An organism is unable to return, even partially, to a previous stage already realised in the ranks of its ancestors.*'

The usual example is the human tail; we all used to have them when we were apes, but now all we have is a coccyx at the base of the spine and plainly no tail, because we no longer hang from trees. Or there are the gills of whales – the whales evolved from fish and once had gills, but no longer have them and have never regrown them. Dollo never argued himself that his statement was an inviolable 'law' of nature, but it became to be accepted as such.

And then along came frogs with teeth. Several scientists had claimed that there were various species which had re-evolved body parts that had previously disappeared but, in 2010, huge excitement was caused in the scientific world when the South American frog *gastrotheca guentheri* was proven from fossil records to have lost its teeth 230 million years ago and then regained them in the past 20 million years. Scientists are still debating whether that means Dollo's Law is redundant. If so, it means that humans could even have tails again, if only some proper use could be found for them.

DUVERGER'S LAW

Developed by French sociologist and political scientist Michael Duverger, his Law and accompanying hypothesis should have been much under discussion in Britain in the early part of 2011 – except that no one dared, at least not in government.

For Duverger concerned himself with voting systems, particularly 'plurality' rule such as the first-past-the-post system. Duverger's Law stated that such systems will tend to become two-party systems. His eponymous hypothesis then stated that countries using proportional representation at the ballot box would tend towards multi-party systems of government.

Duverger's Law has generally been correct in the UK, as the first-past-the-post system has resulted in either Labour or Conservative Governments for more than 60 years. But the system threw up an exceptional result in 2010, in which a Coalition of Conservative and Liberal Democrats formed the Government. Subsequently, as part of their power-sharing deal, a referendum was held on 5 May 2011 to decide whether to switch to a different system of voting, namely the Alternative Vote system. The British public overwhelmingly voted 'no'.

It was still 'plurality' rule, however. For what the Coalition did not do was allow any discussion of proportional representation, so Duverger's name was never mentioned. Whether his Law becomes better known in future remains to be seen.

FINAGLE'S LAW

Also known as Finagle's Corollary to Murphy's Law, Finagle's Law of Dynamic Negatives states that *'anything that can go wrong will go wrong, and at the worst possible time'*. There is also a second Finagle's Law, much loved of modern computer geeks: *'The perversity of the Universe tends towards a maximum.'*

The creation of Finagle's Law is usually ascribed to John W Campbell (1910–71), the highly influential editor of science-fiction magazines. Like any good journalist, he never revealed his sources, so we do not know where he got the name from, or even if there was a Mr or Mrs Finagle. We do know, however, that science-fiction author Larry Niven took the Finagle name and gave it to a god in his stories about miners on asteroids. The deity Finagle had a prophet called Murphy, which undoubtedly meant Niven was having a joke at the Laws' expense.

FLANAGAN'S PRECEPT

We've all heard of Murphy's Law, which in its briefest form states that *'anything that can go wrong will go wrong'*. Flanagan's Precept states simply this: *'Murphy was an incurable optimist.'*

Sadly, we do not know who Flanagan was, or if he or she ever wrote anything else as humorous or as perspicacious as the Precept.

GATES' LAW

According to Microsoft founder Bill Gates (b. 1955), the speed of software halves every 18 months. As he is one of the world's richest men, he must be right. Or was he just having a laugh?

It is similar to Wirth's Law promulgated by Niklaus Emil Wirth (b. 1934), the Swiss computer genius, who stated in 1995: *'Software is getting slower more rapidly than hardware becomes faster.'*

Another computing Law is Moore's, named after Gordon E Moore (b. 1929), the founder of Intel. It states: *'The number of transistors that can be placed inexpensively on an integrated circuit doubles approximately every two years.'* Moore first stated his findings in the 1960s, and he has been proven right in every decade since.

GODWIN'S LAW

Mike Godwin is possibly the youngest person ever to promulgate a Law which is also one of the best known of the computer age. Godwin was still in his early thirties when he wrote: *'As an online discussion grows longer, the probability of a comparison involving Nazis or Hitler approaches 1.'*

In other words, in any online discussion, sooner or later a contributor will say that another contributor's actions or beliefs can be compared to those of Adolf Hitler and his Nazi party.

A noted lawyer and author, Godwin made his statement as a form of protest against the trivialisation of debate on the Internet. Yet, in typical fashion for the worldwide web, his own Law is now the subject of fierce debate. And yes,

Godwin's Law itself has been compared to Nazi censorship. You couldn't make it up.

HANNAN'S LAW

Developed after years of journalistic cynicism gained from analysing pronouncements by politicians and celebrities, my Law is a simple observation about the likelihood of anyone in public life actually telling the truth: *'A statement has less credibility the more exaggeratedly someone states it.'*

Watch any party political broadcast and judge it against reality, or read the headlines about some celebrity pledging undying love to another and you will soon realise my Law is sound. Will it ever catch on?

HANLON'S RAZOR

(*See* **Occam's Razor** *below*)

Very much in the spirit of Occam's Razor, this eponymous Law states: *'Never attribute to malice that which is adequately explained by stupidity.'*

So says the 'razor', which was attributed to Robert J Hanlon in 1980, but which might, in fact, have been coined by science-fiction author Robert A Heinlein almost 40 years previously. In *Logic of Empire*, Heinlein wrote, 'you have attributed conditions to villainy that simply result from stupidity'.

Hanlon's version is contained in *Murphy's Law, Book Two: More Reasons Why Things Go Wrong* by Arthur Bloch. Hanlon or Heinlein, it's a pretty smart razor, though not one that conspiracy theorists enjoy.

MURPHY'S LAW

The most famous of the eponymous laws is named after a real person. Captain Edward Murphy (1918–90) was a development engineer working at Muroc army airfield, now Edwards Air Force Base, in California. An instrument for measuring G-forces on test pilots failed to record a reading, and, although Murphy's exact words are the subject of debate, he came out with a statement to the effect that *'if someone can do a job wrong, it will be done wrong'*. The officer in charge of the project repeated the phrase at a press conference, crediting it to Murphy, and it was picked up by technical journals of the day.

By the time it reached popular usage, the Law had been subtly altered to read *'Anything that can go wrong will go wrong.'*

Ed Murphy did not have too much go wrong on him after he left the military. He ended up working on life-support and safety systems for the Apollo spacecraft.

Muphry's Law – note the spelling – is a variation of Murphy's Law which states that, if you write something critical of editing or proofreading, there will be a mistake in what you have written.

OCCAM'S RAZOR

'Entities must not be multiplied beyond necessity.' So wrote William of Ockham, an English Franciscan friar who is believed to have lived from around 1288 to 1348. That was an exciting time in the history of the pre-Reformation Christian Church, when a thinker and philosopher like William could end up in prison or even be burned at the stake

for simply stating beliefs that were deemed to be contrary to Church teaching.

William was indeed charged with heresy and excommunicated in 1327, managing to escape with his life from the papal court by taking refuge with the sympathetic King Louis IV of Bavaria. William's reputation as a leading philosopher of the day was restored after his death when the findings against him were cancelled by a subsequent pope. His Razor – so called because he sliced through obfuscation to get to the nub of a matter – is probably best rendered as '*the simplest explanation is usually the correct one*'.

Sherlock Holmes is the best-known literary exponent of the razor, while it is also stated by the analytical Franciscan friar William of Baskerville, the hero of Umberto Eco's novel *The Name of the Rose*, whose name is a tribute to both William of Ockham and Holmes, whose most famous case was the Hound of the Baskervilles.

PARETO PRINCIPLE

It was the management consultant JM Juran (1904–2008) who suggested that this principle, often expressed as '*the vital few and the trivial many*' be named after Vilfredo Pareto (1848–1923), an Italian economist, philosopher and engineer.

In 1906, Pareto observed that 80 per cent of Italy was owned by just 20 per cent of the people, and that 80:20 ratio turned out to apply to a lot of economic activity as well.

He showed that, in all societies at all times, wealth was not distributed fairly, and this led him to conclude that this happened because of human nature.

In later life, Pareto was much admired by Mussolini which made him a controversial figure in Italy.

PARKINSON'S LAW

One of the most famous of all such Laws, it is usually stated as '*work expands so as to fill the time available for its completion*'. It was first stated by British writer and naval historian Professor Cecil Northcote Parkinson (1909–93) in a not entirely humorous essay which appeared in the *Economist* magazine in 1955.

Parkinson arrived at his conclusion after years of watching how the British Civil Service operated. The satirical attack, full of equations on how the civil service cooked up meaningless jobs, struck a chord with the public, and three years later he brought out *Parkinson's Law* which became a best-seller and enabled him to give up being an academic and become a full-time writer.

PETER PRINCIPLE

Dr Laurence J Peter (1919–90) was a Canadian psychologist who also looked at the way companies and organisations work. His theory was that '*every new member in a hierarchical organisation climbs the hierarchy until they reach their level of maximum incompetence*'. In other words, if you keep getting promoted, eventually you'll be in a job you can't do. Scott Adam based his Dilbert Principle (see above) on Peter's dictum.

STIGLER'S LAW

This Law is very apposite for this book, for it deals with

eponyms. More correctly known as Stigler's Law of Eponymy, it states: *'No scientific discovery is named after its original discoverer.'* It's a bit sweeping, but the general drift must be accurate as the man who framed it is one of the world's leading researchers into such material.

Professor Stephen Stigler published his Law in 1980 while working at the University of Chicago where, at the time of writing, he is Ernest DeWitt Burton Distinguished Service Professor of Statistics in the Department of Statistics. He is as renowned for his statistical expertise on sports such as baseball and golf as he is on pure statistics.

Stigler's contention of 30 years ago came from meticulous observation of the scientific world. He sent me a copy of the paper in which he formulated the Law, and its assertions are borne out in this book. Sometimes people just do not get the credit for what they did, and someone else – perhaps a richer or more famous person, a boss or employer, or just someone with a grasp of good public relations – butts in and puts their name on a discovery or invention.

Perhaps the most famous example is Halley's Comet, which was discovered by astronomers in China and Babylon long before the birth of Christ. Halley's Comet proves the theory that eponyms are creatures that follow no Laws, except Stigler's.

STURGEON'S LAW

The American author Theodore Sturgeon (1918–85) got so fed up in 1951 defending his and other writers' science-fiction that he retaliated: *'90 per cent of science-fiction is crap, but then 90 per cent of film, literature, consumer goods, etc. are crap.*' He did not say whether that ratio included his own work.

In a life in which he had a host of jobs from sailor to hotelier to screenwriter, Sturgeon gained everlasting science-fiction fame as the man who introduced the phrase 'live long and prosper' into *Star Trek*.

SUTTON'S LAW

A fairly recent medical Law which states that, when diagnosing, always consider the obvious. It is named after Willie Sutton (1901–80), an infamous bank robber in the USA who was reputed to have been asked why he robbed banks and replied, 'Because that's where the money is.' Sutton later denied saying it, asserting that a journalist made it up, but he definitely did say, 'You can't rob a bank on charm and personality.'

Though he robbed 100 banks, often in disguise, and frequently broke out of prison, Sutton became an American Robin Hood, as he reportedly would not rob a bank if there was a baby inside and, although he carried guns, he claimed they weren't loaded 'because someone might get hurt'.

THOMAS THEOREM

An American sociologist, William Isaac Thomas (1863–1957) published his famous theorem in 1928: '*If men define situations as real, they are real in their consequences.*' Or, put another way, if we believe something is real, we will act as if it is real, and it will be real. It is sometimes expressed as: '*If people think someone is great, then he is great.*'

There have been many examples to prove his theorem's

validity, with Orson Welles's *War of the Worlds'* panic in 1938 one of the best known. Thomas himself led an interesting life, his academic career being damaged in 1918 when he was charged under the Mann Act with transporting a woman across State boundaries for immoral purposes – he was caught by the FBI with the wife of an army officer who was serving in France. Thomas was acquitted, although the prosecution, the banner headlines and that fact that he held left-wing views cost him professorships.

WEINER'S LAW OF LIBRARIES

'There are no answers, only cross references.' So check him out yourself.

·6·

NATURAL SELECTION

FLORA AND FAUNA

With dozens of new species of animal life being found every day, scientists have long ago run out of 'proper scientific' names for them, which is why there is a species of frog named after pop star Sting, various insects named after American Presidents – some Presidents, perhaps, being more appropriately 'insectoid' than others – and spiders named after everybody from Harrison Ford to Nelson Mandela.

The following list is very much a selection of genii and species named after people. Undoubtedly the greatest influence in the field of naming animals and plants was Carl Linnaeus (1707–78) of Sweden, the Father of Toxonomy (the science of classification) and Prince of Botanists, whose system for naming, ranking and classifying every living thing has been in use for more than 200 years.

ABELIA

This eponymous shrub commemorates a glorious failure and a terribly British piece of fair play. The Abelia genus of up to 30 species of shrubs is part of the honeysuckle family – of which the best known is the Chinese Abelia – which is named after Dr Clarke Abel (1789–1826), an English surgeon and naturalist. Abel left his practice in Brighton to accompany William Pitt Amherst, later an Earl and the Governor-General of India, on a diplomatic mission to China in 1816. Amherst refused to kowtow to the Emperor, and he and his party were ordered out of China, and then suffered a shipwreck on the way home. Abel had collected plants and seeds from Chinese gardens, but they were lost in the wreck. Abel had left duplicates in Canton, and using these he was able to show the plant was a type of honeysuckle. Still, it was not a successful outcome to the trip.

In 1844, Scottish botanist Robert Fortune (1812–80), the man who brought tea plants from China to India, managed to transport living Abelia plants to Britain and they soon became popular.

Abel had died in 1826 aged just 37, but, as the man who had found the plant and described it, his name and not Fortune's was attached to this enduringly popular shrub. In true sporting fashion, Fortune himself thought it only right that Abel should be honoured, and you should not feel too sorry for him – there are many species of tree and plant called '*fortunei*' after him.

ABBOTT'S BOOBY

This seabird, unfortunately now endangered, is found in and

around Christmas Island. It is one of a number of species named after Dr William Louis Abbott (1860–1936), an American physician and naturalist who travelled the world finding and describing new species of flora and fauna.

ARACHNID

Which came first – the legend or the name? In ancient mythology, Arachne was a weaver who boasted that she was better at her skill than Pallas Athene, the goddess known to the Romans as Minerva.

When Arachne produced a tapestry so beautiful that not even a divine weaver could surpass it, the goddess reacted in the tetchy manner displayed by so many residents of Olympus, and turned Arachne into a spider. Which is an interesting coincidence, as the Greek word for spider is *arachne*. Whether the poor lass gave her name to the creatures, or vice versa, is lost in unwritten history.

BANKSIA

There are around 170 types of Banksia, a genus of plants found originally in Australia. Their name commemorates Sir Joseph Banks (1743–1820), an English naturalist and explorer who has some 80 species named after him. He was a member of Captain Cook's first voyage, and his descriptions of flora and fauna found on the trip made him famous. His name is attached to several areas of several countries, including Banks in the Australian capital Canberra, and his face was once emblazoned on an Australian $5 note.

BARTLETT PEAR

Actually, it's a Williams Pear … or more than a hundred other names around the world. Enoch Bartlett (1799–1860) was not even the originator of the variety which bears his name, as he merely bought the farm on which they were growing and named the pear trees after himself. It was not until 1828 that it was realised that Bartlett's Pears were the same as the Williams Bon Chrétien variety, which had been imported from England. Yet Enoch Bartlett's pears were delicious and became by far the most popular variety in Canada and the USA, where they retain old Enoch's moniker.

BEGONIA

These perennial flowers are named after Michel Bégon (1638–1710) who did nothing to find or describe the genus but was a passionate collector of plants who also happened to be Governor of Haiti. The great French botanist Charles Plumier (1646–1704) described the plant in his massive tome on the plants of the Americas, attaching the name of 'Bégon' to it in honour of his fellow Frenchman.

BOUGAINVILLEA

Native to South America but long ago transplanted to warm countries worldwide, this genus of plants was first described in Brazil by French botanist Philibert Commerçon (1727–73), also known as Commerson, who accompanied Louis-Antoine, Comte de Bougainville (1729–1811) on his voyage around the world from 1766 to 1769 and named the genus after him.

Bougainville had a stellar career as an admiral, an army

marshal, a best-selling author and a member of the French Academy of Sciences, while Commerçon was also a colourful figure as his supposed young male servant on the voyage turned out to be his mistress, Jeanne Baré. As women were banned from the French and most other navies, she was probably the first woman to circumnavigate the globe.

CAMELLIA

Named by Linnaeus in honour of George Kamel (1661–1706), a Jesuit priest who was also a botanist and who greatly enlarged European knowledge of Asian floral species during his mission to the Marianas and Philippines.

CINCHONA

If history is written by the victors, eponyms are often written by the unctuous.

Not even the great Linnaeus was immune, as he named this genus of shrubs after the Countess of Chinchon in Spain, somehow missing the first 'h' in her name.

Even though other people had previously described the genus and the vital use of cinchona bark as a source of quinine, Linnaeus preferred the story about how the Countess, the wife of the Spanish viceroy, had been cured of malarial symptoms by the traditional native use of the bark.

The trouble is that there is no confirmation of the Countess's story which, don't forget, happened more than a hundred years before Linnaeus gave the genus her name. It seems that, once again, an aristocrat's name was attached to something because that was the 'done thing' in those days.

COX'S ORANGE PIPPIN

Despite its name, this fruit is an apple, and gets its name from the horticulturalist Richard Cox who had been a brewer and had retired to Colnbrook, formerly in Buckinghamshire but now in Berkshire. There he successfully created a hybrid of a Ribston Pippin and Blenheim Orange in the 1820s.

DAHLIA

The national flower of Mexico is named in honour of a Swede, the botanist Ander Dahl (1751–89). Spanish botanist Antonio José Cavanilles gave the genus its name in late 1789 after learning of the death of Dahl just a few months previously.

DOUGLAS FIR

More correctly this famous tree should be named Douglas-fir to indicate that it is not strictly a fir tree. It was named after David Douglas (1799–1834), a Scottish botanist who successfully introduced several species of tree and plant to his native land, including the Sitka Spruce and the Lupin. He was killed at the age of 35 on an expedition to Hawaii, falling into an animal pit trap whereupon a bull fell on top of him.

FAUNA

The very word 'fauna' is itself an eponym. Meaning the animal life of a place or era, the word derives ultimately from the Greek god Pan. In Roman usage, this god of wild places became Faunus, and he had a wife, daughter or sister called Fauna who had many divine traits such as foretelling the future, but was more revered in several guises as the mother of wild things. Carl Linnaeus (1707–78), the Prince of Botanists, popularised the word in the title of his second book *Fauna Suecica*, a description of Swedish animal life published in 1746, which became the template for the work of all naturalists.

FLORA

That man Linnaeus again. His first book, *Flora Suecica*, published in 1744, made popular the name of the Latin goddess of flowers, Flora, as a description of the plant life of a place or time. The word had already been in common use among writers and botanists for many decades, but the mark of approval by the great Linnaeus saw 'flora' adopted as the standard word.

FREESIA

Native to Africa, this genus was named in honour of a German doctor, Friedrich Heinrich Theodor Freese (1795–1876), by his friend the Danish botanist Christian Friedrich Ecklon (1795–1868). Ecklonia, a genus of kelp, is named after the latter gentleman.

GARDENIA

Dr Alexander Garden (1730–91) left his native Scotland for the USA when his father, also Alexander, was appointed rector of the Episcopalian church in Charleston, South Carolina. A keen botanist, Garden was impressed by the work of Linnaeus and sent many plant and animal specimens to Sweden for his examination. In reluctant thanks for his help, Linnaeus named the plant sometimes known as Cape jasmine after Garden, despite the fact that it hails from southern Africa and had no American connection.

GENTIAN

This genus of more than 400 plants is named after Gentius, the last king of Illyria, which was located roughly where Albania and Croatia are now. Before the Romans defeated him in battle, took over his kingdom and dragged him off to exile, Gentius was credited with discovering that the roots of bitterwort, a species of Gentian, had tonic properties. That man Linnaeus had heard the story and gave the genus its name in 1753.

GREENGAGE

A type of plum, the greengage is named after Sir William Gage, 7th baronet of that name, who brought them into Britain in 1724. To be honest, it's a bit of a cheat that the fruit is so named, because the French had been cultivating them for centuries.

In France, greengages are known by their original name – Reine Claude – as they were called after Claude, Duchess of Brittany, who was known as 'the good queen' and was consort of King Francis I of France in the early 16th century. When Gage or a relative, the Rev John Gage, brought them to Britain, the labels identifying the Reine Claude plums somehow got lost and, as they were green and belonged to Sir William Gage, the fruit acquired a new name. No one said eponyms have to be honest.

FUCHSIA

The French botanist Charles Plumier (1646–1704) was a monk who made three plant-finding expeditions to the West Indies. In 1703, he found a new genus of flowering plants on the island of Hispaniola, now Haiti and the Dominican Republic, and he named it in honour of Leonhart Fuchs (1501–66), the German doctor and academic who is considered to be one of the founders of botanical science. The colour Fuchsia, a purple-red mix, is named after the flower and therefore also gets its name from Leonhart Fuchs.

GUPPY

There is surely not an aquarium or fish tank on the planet which does not contain a guppy. Unusual in that the female of the species is generally larger than the male, guppies are members of the Poeciliidae family which have been bred by aquarists to become spectacularly beautiful, small fish. They also have a short gestation period of about four weeks, meaning they can reproduce frequently which is another reason why they are popular with fish keepers.

Born in London in 1836 and brought up in a castle by his grandparents, Lechmere Guppy enjoyed a tumultuous life before settling in Trinidad where his father Robert had been Mayor of San Fernando.

Having left England at the age of 18, he survived his ship being wrecked on the coast of New Zealand and settled down to live for two years with the local Maoris – so much so that the local chief almost married his daughter to Guppy. He managed to avoid the marriage and, with Maori tattoos as a souvenir, he moved to Trinidad where he developed his self-taught talents in geology and palaeontology while working in the Colonial Service.

Around Trinidad, he captured some small unknown fish and sent them to the British Museum for examination, where the curator of zoology, a Dr Gunther, named them *girardinus guppii* in his honour.

As we have seen with other eponyms, someone else had actually found the guppy first and, indeed, Wilhelm C Peters had named them *poecilia reticulata* which is now accepted as the given name of the species.

Nevertheless, Guppy had remained in the Latin name long enough for Lechmere's surname to become the public's chosen name for this popular little fish.

JOHN DORY

It is monumentally ugly, it has far too many fins and bones in relation to its tasty flesh, but this fish has always been prized by chefs who appreciate its delicacy. Also known as the St Pierre fish, once again we have a problem with a disputed derivation, because John Dory may or may not have been a genuine person.

The golden skin of the fish found mostly in the Mediterranean may account for one possible reason why it is called 'John Dory', since the French word for yellow is '*jaune*' and for golden is '*dorée*'. But this is a book of eponyms and we much prefer the version which says that the John Dory was called after the lead character in an old folk ballad which celebrated a ship captain of that name from Cornwall who took on the French pirates and roundly defeated them.

Captain John Dory has been lost in the mists of time, but a John Dory fillet, preferably pan fried in a little white wine and garlic, and washed down with a potent Chablis, keeps his name alive in memorable fashion.

LOGANBERRY

John Harvey Logan (1841–1928) was a district attorney and judge whose hobby was botany. In 1886, he was trying to improve the local blackberries in his home town of Santa Cruz, California, when he accidentally planted a bush beside a raspberry bush. He was able to grow the resultant hybrid from seed, and the loganberry began its life.

It has mostly been used for growing other hybrids such as the tayberry and the boysenberry, which is a cross between a raspberry, blackberry and loganberry and gets its name from Rudolph Boysen (1895–1950), on whose fruit farm in California it was first grown in the 1920s.

MCINTOSH APPLES

When next you eat a McIntosh Red apple, consider that it and every other apple of the name is a direct descendant from one tree in Ontario, Canada, cultivated by farmer John McIntosh (1777–1846).

McIntosh was the son of Scottish parents who went north from his home in New York State and settled in what is now South Dundas township. He found seedlings on the land, and one single apple tree grew from them, which eventually produced the red apples he named McIntosh Red after himself. No one knows how the seedlings got there in an area not renowned for any kind of apples. The tree stood until

1910 and a plaque now marks the spot. The Apple Macintosh computer is indeed named after the fruit, so John McIntosh has his name well and truly immortalised.

MAGNOLIA

Another name that came from Charles Plumier's visit to the West Indies (see *Begonia* and *Fuchsia* above). The genus Magnolia, which has over 200 species, was found by Plumier on Martinique and he named it in honour of Pierre Magnol (1638–1715), Director of France's Royal Botanic Garden who devised the concept of plant families.

PÈRE DAVID'S DEER

Once a wild species that roamed China, the only remaining Père David's Deer are now in captivity, the species being officially declared extinct in the wild in October 2008. Yet were it not for a few deer being kept in the Imperial Hunting Park in Beijing in China in the 19th century, the species would be completely extinct.

It was in the park that they were seen by Father Jean Pierre Armand David CM (1826–1900), a French missionary of the Lazarist order, more formally known as the Congregation of the Mission. Père David, a self-taught zoologist, botanist and mineralogist, kept coming back to the unusual-looking deer during his long stay in China.

Much of his time in China and his extensive explorations were paid for by the French Government who were delighted with his discoveries – no wonder, as he became famous for finding the Giant Panda in Sichuan Province in 1869. He was also able to send a description of the deer back to France in 1865 and, later, other deer were exported to the West by gift of the Emperor, while a few were smuggled out. Just as well, because, when the Boxer rebellion broke out in 1899 long after Père David had gone home, the few remaining deer were eaten by the besieged European and Japanese troops in the Imperial City.

Enter the 11th Duke of Bedford, a prominent naturalist who has several animal species named after him and who was determined to build up a herd of the deer at his Woburn Abbey home. The other examples of the species in Europe were sent to Woburn and a successful breeding programme took place. With hundreds of the deer at Woburn, in 1986, Père David's Deer were reintroduced to China at their old stomping ground, the Imperial Hunting Park. The plan is gradually to reintroduce them to the wild in preserved areas of China.

POINSETTIA

Otherwise known as *euphorbia pulcherrima* or *noche buena* (Christmas Eve Flower), the plant is named after the man who introduced it to the USA, Joel Roberts Poinsett (1779–1851), who was fortunate to be able to indulge his botany hobby while acting as an ambassador for the USA.

A quite remarkable fellow, as a young man, Poinsett inherited a fortune and used it to travel through Europe and Asia, becoming the first American to visit several countries and territories. Czar Alexander tried to persuade him to stay and join the Russian Government, but Poinsett went home to South Carolina where he became a diplomat, specialising in Latin America, where he made extensive embassies to

Chile and Argentina. He then represented South Carolina in Congress before being appointed the USA's first Minister to Mexico.

It was in Mexico that he found the plant which bears his name, and sent it home to the USA where it became very popular in a short space of time. Poinsett later served as Secretary for War during the time of the Second Seminole War in Florida.

PRZEWALSKI'S HORSE

Once extinct in the wild, this species of horse native to central Asia is being reintroduced in Mongolia. Also known as the Asian or Mongolian Wild Horse, it is one of the few truly wild equine species and has never been domesticated. It is named after the explorer Nikolai Mikhailovich Przhewalsky (1839–88), who was a bit of a wild man himself, known for always carrying a whip in one hand and a rifle in the other. His five major expeditions opened up Central Asia, and he once got to within 150 miles of Lhasa in the forbidden kingdom of Tibet. He brought back thousands of plant and animal species to Russia, and was rewarded with high honours by the Imperial Court.

The spelling of 'Przewalski' is due to his family being Polish. In the Russian spelling, he has dozens of plants named after him, as well as the village of Przhevalskoye in Smolensk Oblast, Russia, which has a museum dedicated to him.

Due to a remarkable facial similarity, a myth grew up that Joseph Stalin was his illegitimate son, but, wild man though he was, Przhewalsky was not in Georgia nine months before Stalin was born to a cobbler named Jughashvili.

SEQUOIA

The name for the redwood species of giant trees, some of which are the world's largest and certainly tallest living organisms, comes from a famous Native American, Sequoyah. Son of a Virginian fur trader called Nathaniel Gist and the daughter of a Cherokee chief, Sequoyah was known as George Gist or Guess in English, but preferred Sequoyah.

Though he travelled extensively across the USA, he never actually saw the trees named after him, nor did he visit California where Sequoia National Park is located. Yet he was a leader to the Cherokee people and much admired and respected by the white people among whom he lived, first practising his trade as a silversmith then joining the US forces to combat the British in the war of 1812.

He achieved lasting fame by painstakingly creating a form of writing for the Cherokee, who had not previously had any letters or alphabet. Sequoyah made a syllabary of 85 characters, each of which stands for a syllable in the Cherokee language. Though at first he was accused of witchcraft, within a few years, Sequoyah's system had enabled the entire Cherokee nation to be transformed by literacy.

It is believed to be the only time that a single human being has created a written language that was adopted by an entire nation and, to this day, the Cherokee use his syllabary without alteration.

It was truly a feat that was giant, rather like the trees that bear Sequoyah's name.

THOMSON'S GAZELLE

One of the loveliest animals on the planet with its distinctive black stripe between a russet coat and white belly, this gazelle is named after James Thomson (1858–95), the Scottish-born explorer who made several expeditions through Africa and was the first man to prove that Kilimanjaro had snow at its peak. He was said to be partly the inspiration for the Captain Good character in the novel *King Solomon's Mines* by H Rider Haggard, as Thomson, like Good, frightened off native warriors by taking out his false teeth.

Unlike other explorers of the time, Thomson also managed to conduct his expeditions without killing any Africans.

WISTERIA

Made even more famous by American television series *Desperate Housewives*, who all live on Wisteria Lane, this genus of climbing plants was named after Dr Caspar Wistar (1761–1818), an American of German extraction and a very interesting character. He came from a wealthy family of glassmakers in Philadelphia, and thus was able to study medicine at the University of Edinburgh, having been inspired to become a doctor by the carnage he saw while serving as a nurse at the Battle of Germantown in 1777.

In Edinburgh, he met many of the Scots who were leading the Enlightenment at that period, including James Boswell (see *Boswellian*, chapter 1). Returning to his native city, Wistar became both a medical doctor and professor of chemistry and later anatomy at what became the University of Pennsylvania.

Though a lifelong Quaker, Wistar was not always a

peaceful sort, for he fought at least one duel. His brilliant mind saw him become expert in a whole range of sciences, including botany, and he succeeded Thomas Jefferson, no less, as President of the American Philosophical Society. He also became President of the Society for the Abolition of Slavery.

When botanist Thomas Nuttall travelled west and became the first man to describe this native American species, he named it after Wistar whom he had met in Philadelphia. The spelling variation was apparently due to a misprint in an early book, but proof that Wistar is the source of the eponym is that many people called the plant 'Wistaria' afterwards.

Some sources say Wisteria is named after Charles Wister of Grumblethorpe in Pennsylvania whose father funded the voyage of the *Empress of China*, the first American ship to visit mainland China, and which brought the Chinese species of the plant to the USA. Caspar Wistar or Charles Wister? It's not worth risking hysteria to worry about Wisteria.

·7·

ALL IN THE BEST POSSIBLE TASTE

Eponyms concocted around recipes, foodstuffs, dishes and diets.

ALBERT PUDDING

This delicious, rich pudding should really be known as Prince Albert's Pudding, and is often called by that name in recipe books. Although we do not know the inventor, it was named in honour of Prince Albert of Saxe-Coburg-Gotha (1819–61), much-loved husband of Queen Victoria, whose name adorns items ranging from an old type of tobacco to the eponymous Memorial and Hall and a city in Saskatchewan, Canada.

ATKINS DIET

Probably the most famous 'diet' of the late 20th century and, like all 'diets', it is a complete misnomer. For diet does not mean a way of losing weight, at least not in its original sense. The word derives from the Greek *'diaita'* meaning 'method of life' and, when 'diet' first came into the English language via Latin and Old French, it meant the totality of what you ate. Diet is still used in that manner, as in 'the diet of the natives consisted of berries', although in modern usage diet almost always means eating in a special way to lose weight, which is why we speak of 'going on a diet'.

One of the most popular such slimming diets in recent years was that invented and popularised by Dr Robert Atkins (1930–2003). Atkins himself preferred to call his diet a 'nutritional approach', and he based it on existing research and his own observations. Basically, he decided that too much carbohydrate was the real culprit in modern eating, and that it caused excess production of insulin among other problems.

His own switch to a high-protein diet that allowed fatty foods but cut out carbohydrates reduced his weight considerably. His diet was soon in vogue – literally so, as *Vogue* magazine promoted it and soon celebrities were queuing up to go on the Atkins Diet, which he described in a best-selling book in 1972. A multi-million-dollar industry built on books and foodstuffs soon followed for the good doctor, even though he himself actually put on weight again and reportedly weighed 258lb (18st 6lb) or 117kg when he died of head injuries after a fall at the age of 72.

It could be that the Atkins Diet became so popular because it allowed you to eat steak and cheese but, as the scientific basis of the Atkins Diet is still the subject of debate, you are advised to consult your GP before going on any slimming diet.

BATH OLIVER BISCUITS

This biscuit or cracker is named after Dr William Oliver (1695–1764), a physician who treated patients attending the various spas and thermal baths in the English city of Bath in the mid-18th century. He had originally created Bath Buns, derived from the ancient recipe for Bath Cake, but these were too fattening for his patients. Dr Oliver duly came up with the hard, dry cracker and, in his Will, he passed the recipe on to a Mr Atkins (no relation to the diet doctor above). Atkins had been a coachman, but took the recipe and the £100 and ten sacks of wheat flour left to him by Dr Oliver, and made himself a fortune.

BATTENBERG CAKE

This is a real English mystery – why is one of England's most famous and popular cakes called after German aristocrats?

Not one but four princes are commemorated in the name of this delicious concoction of sponge cake, jam and marzipan. Its distinctive four squares of sponge, two coloured pink and two yellow, in a check pattern, represent the German princes Louis, Alexander, Henry and Francis Joseph of Battenberg, who were very popular in several countries of Europe in Victorian times. Prince Louis married Queen Victoria's granddaughter, also Victoria, and became a British citizen, rising to the post of First Sea Lord in the Navy.

It is believed that the cake was created in Germany to mark the marriage of Prince Louis to Princess Victoria of Hesse, but was imported to Britain on a wave of popular warmth towards the dashing young prince.

The strange thing is that, during the First World War, with anti-German feeling running high, Prince Louis retired from his naval post and changed the family name to Mountbatten. Yet, for some reason, the cake remained Battenberg – the British public had grown to love the cake and, as usual, were loath to be politically correct.

Lord Louis Mountbatten, Earl Mountbatten of Burma, was the son of Prince Louis, and distinguished himself with his war service before becoming the last Viceroy of India. Mountbatten, who was killed by an IRA bomb in 1979, always took a personal interest in another remnant of his family's old name, the Battenberg Cup. Presented in 1905 by Prince Louis, the trophy was originally competed for by crews from the US and Royal Navies but, for many years now, the Battenberg Cup has been awarded to the operational ship judged to be the best in the entire US Navy. Like the cake, no one has ever tried to change the cup's name to 'Mountbatten'.

BECHAMEL SAUCE

The classic white sauce that is the base for so many other sauces and dishes was created in, and named after, the household of Louis de Bechamel (1630–1703), the Marquis of Nointel, head steward to the court of King Louis XIV and one of the richest men in 17th-century France. Bechamel was so multi-talented that he may even have invented the sauce himself but, in any case, it was simply a variation of a creamy sauce whose recipe appeared in the founding textbook of French cooking, *Le Cuisinier François*, published in 1651 by the chef Francois Pierre La Varenne. Bechamel was a marquis, and La Varenne merely a chef, so snobbery may have had its part to play in naming this versatile sauce.

BEEF WELLINGTON

The classic British dish of beefsteak coated in pâté surrounded by puff pastry is named after the great Duke, of course. Or is it? For one thing, there is no published recipe for Beef Wellington which bears that name until the 1960s, and there is dispute as to whether the Wellington in the name is Arthur Wellesley, 1st Duke of that name, or Wellington, New Zealand, where the dish was said to have been created for a civic feast. In culinary matters, it is usually best to rely on the French, and filet de boeuf en croûte is an old favourite in that country. Perhaps the Duke had some before Waterloo and brought it home with him?

The Irish have also long had Steak Wellington, and Wellesley was, of course, born in Dublin. It may well be that Beef Wellington is named after the Duke, but how it came to bear his name must remain a mystery. He certainly made no claim to inventing or importing the dish.

Sometimes, sadly, the dish can go wrong and the beef ends up tasting like old wellingtons. Perhaps, then, a disgruntled gourmet gave it the name.

BISMARCK HERRINGS

Herrings cured in a pickle of salt, sugar, vinegar, wine and onions, and traditionally packed tight in barrels and jars, these delicious sea fish are named after the Iron Chancellor, Otto von Bismarck (1815–98). They are evidence that Bismarck, for all his conservative nature and Prussian uprightness, enjoyed a bit of self-promotion. For the merchant who first sold the herrings, Johann Wiechmann of Stralsund, actually sought permission from the chancellor to call them after him. Bismarck graciously agreed, and his popularity as the founder of the German Empire ensured that Bismarck herrings became a best-seller. Having gone out of fashion after the Second World War, they are once again on sale using the original recipe devised by Wiechmann's wife Karoline.

CAESAR SALAD

As well as conquering Gaul, bedding Cleopatra and ruling Rome until he was turned into a human pin cushion on the Ides of March, Julius Caesar supposedly dreamed up a salad of romaine lettuce and croutons lightly covered with shavings of parmesan cheese, Worcestershire sauce, boiled-egg quarters, olive oil, lemon and ground black pepper. Anchovies were optional, since Caesar was not a fan.

It's a good story, except for one problem. The Caesar Salad did not appear until almost 2,000 years after the great Julius croaked '*et tu Brute*' and expired in the Senate of Rome. And Worcestershire, never mind its sauce, did not even exist in those Julian days.

The salad was not even created in Italy, as it owes its name to Cesare Cardini (1896–1956), an Italian who emigrated to the USA and came up with the recipe in either San Diego or Tijuana in Mexico in 1924. His brother Alex claimed authorship, having made such a salad for friends who were pilots – hence the 'Aviator's Salad' as it was sometimes known.

The Caesar Salad name stuck, however. Given the theatricality of the salad being tossed at tableside, it soon became popular among the Hollywood movie mob, and Cardini's hotel and restaurant business flourished as a result.

This 'Caesar' was a clever man. He also invented a salad dressing which made him wealthy, and gained a touch of immortality with the recipe that bears his name. Except that old Julius still wrongly gets the unearned credit for the eponymous salad.

CARPACCIO

Though there are conflicting versions of how this meat starter dish got its name, there is no doubt that it is named after Vittore Carpaccio, the Venetian artist who was born around 1450–60 and died in 1525 or 1526, and whose birth name was Scarpazza. Known also as Carpathius, his work can be found in Venice at the Doge's Palace and in the Uffizi Gallery in Florence.

There are a couple of stories as to how Carpaccio gained the artist's name. In Harry's Bar in Venice, they claim that in 1950 a lady customer, the Countess Amalia Nani Mocenigo, asked for raw meat as she had been advised to eat it by her doctor. The chef duly obliged and owner Giuseppe Cipriani, who served it with mustard, saw some sort of resemblance to the red and beige colours prominent in Carpaccio's paintings of the city which were then on show in Venice, and named the new dish after the artist.

Another version is that a Milanese lady liked raw beef but did not want to be heard ordering it in the very smart Savini restaurant in Milan. The waiter suggested using a code name and apparently looked up and saw a painting by Carpaccio.

Interestingly, the latter restaurant's website makes no great claim to have invented Carpaccio. We do know that there was an exhibition of Carpaccio's art in Venice in 1950, and there's no doubt that the Bellini cocktail, named after another Italian artist was invented at Harry's Bar, so the Venetian establishment looks to have the better claim.

CELERY VICTOR

The head chef at the famous St Francis's Hotel in San Francisco, Victor Hertzler (1875–1931), was born in France and certainly had Gallic flair – he would meet guests wearing a red fez rather than the traditional chef's hat, and wrote recipe books to promote himself. He also named many of his creations after himself, of which the best known is this salad dish with marinated celery as the chief ingredient.

CHATEAUBRIAND

A noted author, credited with founding French romanticism, and a brave soldier as well as a diplomat and a considerable political force in France, François-Rene, Vicomte de Chateaubriand (1768–1848) is nevertheless most famous for lending his name to a piece of beef. That's eponyms for you.

In his lifetime, Chateaubriand was famous, or infamous, both for his writing and for his passionate love life – this despite being married. His political fortunes depended on who was in power at any one time in that turbulent era in France. He managed to earn the gratitude of Napoleon and then annoyed the Emperor so much that he was exiled from Paris. Byron adored him, as did most of the French writers of the 19th century, yet Chateaubriand is now largely forgotten apart from the distinctive cut of tenderloin steak with a sauce created by his chef, Montmireil, and named in his honour.

CHICKEN À LA KING

Like quite a few of the eponyms in this book, there is some dispute as to who this item is named after. One version says 'king' is a corruption of Keene, allegedly because the dish was named after Foxhall Keene (1867–1941), the American Olympian polo player, golfer and racehorse owner. Confusingly, Foxhall's father, JR Keene, may also have been the honouree, this time at Claridge's Hotel in London. How 'Keene' became 'King' is a mystery, but perhaps that was due to snobbery.

Alternatively, the dish may have been named after E Clarke King, wealthy customer at the Brighton Beach Hotel in New York. Except that King was a bit late in the day.

The best claim is for William King, who created a recipe of diced chicken in a cream sauce at the Bellevue Hotel in Philadelphia in the 1890s. This version can boast some provenance, because King's obituaries in 1915 all credited him with the invention, and it appeared in American cookbooks from 1900 onwards. Bill King, be assured, is the man after whom the creamy chicken took its name.

CLEMENTINES

This variety of mandarin orange is said by some horticulturalists to have originated in China, but that would spoil a good story. For the generally accepted version is that grateful orphans in Algeria named their favourite fruit after the monk who created it.

Vital Rodier was a Brother of the Annunciation working at an orphanage in Misserghin, a city in the Oran province of Algeria, in the latter years of the 19th century. He had taken the name Marie-Clement when joining the order. Brother Rodier was working in the citrus orchard owned by the orphanage when – by accident, apparently – he spotted a hybrid fruit among the bushes which he could see was popular with local children as they had been helping themselves. He cultivated this hybrid successfully and fed the resulting fruit to the orphans, who insisted that it be called 'clementine' in his honour.

The only problem with that story is that Church records show that Brother Rodier was an ardent gardener and experimentalist, whose work was well known to the Algerian Horticultural Society. He did indeed discover the hybrid, which may well have been the result of one of his own grafts, but called it the 'mandarinette' since it was so obviously derived from the mandarin orange.

After joining the Holy Ghost Fathers when his order amalgamated with them in 1903, Brother Rodier sadly died a year later, shortly after being awarded the Gold Medal of the Horticultural Society. It was the Society which, 20 years later, officially renamed the mandarinette the 'clementine'.

COBB SALAD

Now a general term for any salad containing hard-boiled egg, avocado and bacon, the original Cobb Salad was a 1930s American creation consisting of those three ingredients plus salad greens, tomatoes, chives, chicken and Roquefort cheese. First served at the original Brown Derby restaurant on Wilshire Boulevard, Hollywood, Los Angeles, the salad was either the work of chef Chuck Wilson or owner Robert Howard Cobb, or perhaps both men. Cobb got the honour of the name, however, and it stuck.

CRÊPE SUZETTE

As if to prove the point about disputed eponyms, here is another in the recipe section which is almost dubious. Furthermore, it is not actually the crêpe which is 'Suzette', it is the flaming beurre which accompanies the pancake.

The version of events which is generally accepted is that the beurre was invented by accident in 1895 in the Café de Paris in Monte Carlo. Henri Charpentier, later a very famous chef, restaurateur and author, but then a young waiter, was serving the Prince of Wales, afterwards King Edward VII, on one of his many trips to France. Charpentier had made up a sauce of sugar, butter, orange zest and orange liqueur before accidentally setting fire to it. Tasting the fried and caramelised sauce, Charpentier found that it was even more delicious after being flambéd, and he risked serving it to the Prince, who, of course, was delighted with the new concoction and gallantly insisted on naming it after a female companion present at the table. We know nothing more about that Suzette but, in an alternative version, the dish was named in honour of the French actress Suzanne Reichenberg, whose stage name was Suzette, after she served crêpes during a role in Paris in 1897.

Those two stories at least date from the time when Crêpes

Suzette began to become popular. Another version is that chef Jean Reboux created and named them after Princess Suzette de Carignan, lover of King Louis XV, but, since the king died in 1774, it seems a trifle early for a dish which did not start appearing in restaurants until the 1890s.

Whoever Suzette was, her crêpes are delicious, and she is immortal now.

DOBOS TORTE

No doubt about the creator of this eponymous cake. Jozsef C Dobos (1847–1924) was the Hungarian confectioner who dreamed up a five-layered cake to show off his talents at the Grand Exhibition in Budapest in 1885. Legend has it that Emperor Franz Joseph I and his wife were the first to taste it. With the revolutionary use of chocolate buttercream, the torte was a sweet sensation and its popularity soon spread throughout Europe.

Budapest still has some of the best cakemakers on the planet, and also several high-class cafés which specialise in serving cakes, of which the Dobos Torte, or 'Dobosh' as it is known there, is among the most delicious, as the author can personally testify.

DOM PERIGNON

A zillion trivia quizzes every year ask the same question: can you name the monk who invented champagne? The answer is duly trotted out – Dom Perignon (1638–1715). Except that the supposedly blind monk lived and died without ever tasting, never mind inventing, the sparkling champagne wine that is now so famously and erroneously thought to be his creation.

These are the facts: there was indeed a monk of the Benedictine order called Dom Perignon. He was cellar master of the abbey of Hautvillers near Epernay in the Champagne region of France. He was responsible for vastly improving the quality of French wine, as his common sense rules about grape cultivation and wine production were published and spread widely.

One of his main concerns in life was to *stop* wine becoming gassy, and his ideas on preventing refermentation, the process which creates carbon dioxide in wine, were to prove vital for generations afterwards. He was not blind and did not invent blind tasting. He did not invent corks for wine bottles, and he most certainly did not invent champagne. The heavy glass bottles which enabled champagne production to take place were actually an English invention and what we now know as champagne did not really become widely produced until the 19th century.

There is no doubting the importance of Dom Perignon in the history of viticulture and viniculture, but later monks at Hautvillers were not above gilding the lily and frankly telling fibs about their greatest monk. The myth that he invented champagne was a bit of PR spin on their behalf.

The man who did so much for wine production was honoured by having a vintage champagne named after him in 1921, and there are many experts who maintain that Dom Perignon, now owned by Moët et Chandon, is the finest vintage champagne that money can buy. The best vintages are regularly sold at auction for thousands of pounds per bottle, which you suspect might have offended the Benedictine monk after whom it is named.

DR PEPPER

You have no doubt seen, heard of or tasted the drink, but who was Dr Pepper? For, though the drink is undoubtedly the invention of an American pharmacist, one Charles Alderton, sadly he did not tell us exactly who he named it after.

First served in Waco, Texas, in 1885, and patented that year, Dr Pepper was originally sold by soda-fountain owner Wade Morrison, so it is not named after him either. The best guess is that Morrison called it after a Dr Charles Pepper whom he knew back in his home state of Virginia. The name certainly survived, and has allowed decades of fun for advertising types playing around with 'pep' and 'pepper'.

DUXELLES

François Pierre La Varenne (1615–78) may have been robbed of the credit for creating Bechamel sauce (see above), but he personally caused one of his most famous dishes not to be named after himself. That's because La Varenne named his creation of a paste of mushrooms, onions, herbs and butter after his employer, the Marquis d'Uxelles, Marshal of France under King Louis XIV.

EARL GREY TEA

Though there are differing accounts of how it got his name, this very popular tea is undoubtedly named after Charles, the 2nd Earl Grey (1764–1846) who was Prime Minister of Great Britain from 1830 to 1834. The recipe is said to have come from China along with a consignment of tea flavoured with bergamot oil. The legend is that an envoy sent east by

Grey saved the life of a Chinese mandarin's son and, in grateful thanks, he gave Grey one of his nation's best-kept secrets. Or else, and rather more plausibly, a Chinese gentleman devised the blend of tea for Earl Grey's wife who had been complaining that the water on their Howick estate in Northumberland was too alkaline to make a palatable 'normal' tea.

It is claimed by themselves that the celebrated tea blenders Jacksons of Piccadilly were given the recipe by the Earl in 1830, the year he became Prime Minister, and they were certainly the first to sell it. The tea is still famous, but hardly anyone remembers that Earl Grey was one of the greatest of 19th-century politicians, responsible for the Reform Act 1932 and the abolition of slavery across the British Empire.

EGGS BENEDICT

Yet another recipe for which there is dispute about the name, although it can be stated categorically that the eponym does not come from either Saint Benedict or the American traitor/British spy hero (delete as you think) Benedict Arnold (see chapter 4). A muffin halved and toasted, topped with ham, poached eggs and hollandaise sauce, Eggs Benedict is certainly an American invention, but there are several claims to the name.

The first and best documented is that, in the famous New York hotel the Waldorf Astoria sometime in the 1890s, a Mr Lemuel Benedict ordered poached eggs on toast, some bacon and hollandaise sauce, and the maître d'hotel, Oscar Tschirsky, liked it so much he put a variation on the menu, substituting toasted muffin and ham for the toast and bacon.

The relatives of Mrs LeGrand Benedict, wife of a 19th-century New York financier, tell it differently. The lady was apparently fed up with the menu at Delmonico's New York restaurant where she dined every Saturday. She and the chef reportedly cooked up the new dish between them and Delmonico's used her name on the menu.

Several other claims have been made by other Benedicts elsewhere in the USA, but these two have the best provenance.

GARIBALDI BISCUIT

Devised by a Scotsman, manufactured by an English company and named after an Italian patriot, the Garibaldi biscuit is a classic example of something getting its name from a hero of the day.

Giuseppe Garibaldi (1807–82) is rightly known as the driving force behind the creation of modern Italy. A brilliant general, tales of his derring-do in South America and Italy had made him famous far beyond his native land, and, when he arrived in Britain at Newcastle-upon-Tyne in 1854, the local people gave him a warm welcome, seeing him as a liberator of ordinary working folk. Garibaldi left after only a month to take part in the Second Italian War of Independence, but such was the impact he made that the British press was full of stories about him from then on so that many more people followed his campaigns.

In 1861, a renowned Scottish biscuit-maker, John Carr, devised a new creation of currants between two thin biscuits for the Peek Frean's company that had begun business in Bermondsey, London, four years previously. The firm named their new and very successful biscuit in honour of Garibaldi and, 150 years later, they are still a firm favourite in Britain and elsewhere.

GRAHAM CRACKERS

Very much an American foodstuff, the Reverend Sylvester Graham (1794–1851) invented these wafers originally made from Graham flour, a wholewheat flour that he devised as part of his crusade to improve the American diet which he blamed for causing all sorts of 'lustful' feelings. There was little chance of anyone's passions being inflamed by a Graham cracker, which were deliberately wholesome and bland.

Modern manufacturers add cinnamon or chocolate to give the crackers some taste. That abomination would surely have driven the Reverend Graham quite crackers.

GRANNY SMITH APPLE

Her name really was Smith and she genuinely was a grandmother. Not only that, but Maria Ann Smith, née Sherwood, was an extraordinary woman who died not knowing that she had created a variety of fruit which the whole world appreciates.

Born into farm service in 1799 in Sussex, England, Maria Sherwood married Thomas Smith, an agricultural labourer, at the age of 19. They had eight children, of whom five were surviving when the Smiths were persuaded by government agents to emigrate to Australia. A further child was born in Sydney where the family settled.

From humble beginnings, the Smiths prospered. They were able to buy a small farm in the Ryde area of Sydney and it was there that Maria and her husband, who were both knowledgeable in the propagation of fruits and plants, created an orchard which was soon the envy of the area.

Granny Smith cultivated one particular sort of apple, which she claimed was the product of seedlings produced by French crab apples grown in Tasmania. It had a tart taste, and was never sold commercially for many years. Yet when it was refined for sale, it eventually swept the world.

Granny Smith died in 1870, but local apple growers championed her apple as a 'cooking apple', although by the start of the 20th century it was prized for eating as well. The Granny Smith is still one of the best apple varieties for cooking and eating.

HARVEY WALLBANGER

The delicious mixture of vodka, Galliano and orange juice takes its name from a Mr Harvey, who may or may not have banged into walls. What we don't know is who Harvey really was.

It is quite maddening that we cannot say for certain how one of the world's most famous cocktails got its name. One story is repeatedly told – that the cocktail was invented in California in the 1950s by Donato 'Duke' Antone, founder of the USA's first school of mixology, as cocktail-making is properly termed. Mr Antone certainly knew his mixing – he definitely invented the Rusty Nail, the Flaming Caesar and the Duke, modestly called after himself.

But what of the Harvey Wallbanger? The orange-flavoured drink was supposedly created in Antone's Blackwatch Bar – named in honour of the Scottish regiment that he had fought alongside in the Second World War – in

Los Angeles in the 1950s. The bar is no longer there, although there is an excellent Scottish-themed pub called the Black Watch in Huntington, LA.

Antone apparently took a screwdriver – that's vodka and orange juice to the uninitiated – and added Galliano liqueur, perhaps in homage to his Italian antecedents. It is said the new drink was then consumed in some quantity by a surfer named Tom Harvey who ended up bouncing off the walls on the way out of the bar.

We know Mr Antone's history for certain – he was a genuine war hero, winner of two Silver Stars, two Purple Hearts and a Croix de Guerre. After a long and successful career in mixology, he died in Hartford, Connecticut, in 1992.

Harvey, however, remains elusive. Despite many searches, no one has ever found him or can trace anyone who knew him. What is true is that, in the 1970s, the Galliano marketing people had great fun spreading the story of Harvey the surfer, and even invented a Harvey Wallbanger party game. You can see a version of it online even now.

Could it be that Galliano took Antone's cocktail and added their own spin? We'll probably never know, so, in the spirit of the Wild West (c.f. *The Man Who Shot Liberty Valance*), we can say that the legend has become fact, so we have printed the legend.

KAISER ROLLS

Invented in Vienna, and a descendant of bread rolls that had been popular for centuries, these crusty rolls are thought to have been named in honour of Kaiser (Emperor) Franz

Joseph I (1830–1916), the first Emperor of the Austro-Hungarian Empire, who was much admired by the people of Austria.

Traditionally, there are five 'spokes' on the top of the roll, signifying his five kingdoms – Austria, Hungary, Bohemia, Serbia and Croatia. It was his nephew and heir, Archduke Franz Ferdinand, whose assassination provoked the First World War, after which the title of Kaiser no longer existed in Germany or Austria, though the rolls survive there and elsewhere.

ST HONORÉ CAKE

Gâteau St Honoré is named after the patron saint of bakers and confectioners, Saint Honoré, who was bishop of Amiens in the 6th century. The saint didn't actually do any baking himself, and really only became famous long after he died, when a chapel was built in his name in Paris in the 13th century and the guild of bakers made it their church. The church gave its name to the Rue du Faubourg Saint-Honoré and it was there in 1846 that a cakemaker named Chiboust used two types of pastry and whipped cream to make the cake that he named after the saint and the street on which he worked.

JULES VERNE SAUCE

Jules Verne (1828–1905) was latterly the most famous author of his day, which is why this sauce was named after him, although some claim that he invented it. In which case, he may also have invented the sole, meat dishes, breasts of partridge and garnish which also bear his name, though more likely their creators gave them their names after reading references to such dishes in Verne's novels – he regularly mentioned entire menus.

KUNG PAO CHICKEN

A classic dish of Chinese cuisine, chicken Kung Pao (also spelled as Kung Po and Kung Bao in English) was created in Sichuan province and named in honour of Ding Baozhen, the Governor of the province from 1876 to his death in 1886. He was much loved by the people of the province as a fair and effective ruler on behalf of the Qing dynasty, and the dish comes from his official title of Gong Bao, meaning 'guardian of the palace'.

LAMINGTONS

If you want to start an argument among Australians – never a difficult thing to do – just ask them where 'Lammies' were invented. There is little doubt in Australian minds that these small sponge cakes coated in chocolate icing and desiccated coconut are named after Charles Baillie, Lord Lamington, Governor of Queensland from 1896 to 1901, and that Lammies first saw the light of day somewhere in Queensland – they are an officially designated icon of the State.

The story goes that the Governor's cook was caught unawares by some unexpected visitors and revitalised some stale cake by dipping it in chocolate and coconut, then fed them to His Lordship and guests, and Lamington became a huge fan. It's just a pity that some researcher uncovered an alleged statement by Lord Lamington referring to 'these bloody poofy, woolly biscuits' which were served at State banquets.

Along came more revisionists suggesting that Lamington should really be Lemmington or Leamington and that they originated in New Zealand, while the *Sunday Post* newspaper in Scotland has reported claims that the cake originally came from Lamington in Lanarkshire, a farmer's wife having brought the recipe all the way Down Under from her home village.

Wherever they came from – and Queensland has to be the best bet – Lammies are more popular than ever in Australia as they are used in raising funds for charities.

Lord Lamington, it should be said, was not always a popular chap in Australia, as he once committed the unforgivable sin of shooting a koala bear.

MARGARITA

Tequila, triple sec and lime juice make a delicious Mexican combination, and such is its popularity that at least eight or nine 'Margaritas' lay claim to having it named after them. Indeed, there are too many to detail here, but the most enduring story is that the cocktail was invented in the 1930s or early 1940s by Enrique Bastate Gutierrez in Tijuana, Mexico, just across the border from California, and named by him in honour of his favourite actress Rita Hayworth (1918–87) whose real name was Margarita Carmen Cansino, her father being a Spanish flamenco dancer.

MELBA TOAST

Australia's first great soprano Dame Nellie Melba (1861–1931) was born Helen Porter Mitchell, the daughter of Scottish immigrants in Richmond, Victoria. Her father and first husband tried to prevent her from taking up a singing career, but Nellie went to Melbourne, from which she acquired her stage name, and from there she conquered the world with her ravishing soprano voice.

She was at one time the world's most popular recording artist and, despite the earlier scandal of divorce from her husband – she had an affair with the Duke of Orleans – was made a Dame in 1918 for her tireless charity work in the First World War.

In London in the 1890s, the chef Auguste Escoffier created a dessert of peaches, raspberry sauce and vanilla ice cream in her honour, and called it Peach Melba. Later, Escoffier also invented a variation on humble toasted bread, which he also named after her, hence Melba Toast.

MORNAY SAUCE

A rich Bechamel sauce (see above) with cheese, Mornay sauce is named after the French aristocratic family, but whether it was the Duke, Marquis or Count de Mornay we cannot tell for certain.

OMELETTE ARNOLD BENNETT

The English novelist Arnold Bennett (1867–1931) was at the height of his fame when he stayed at the Savoy Hotel in London. He wanted a dish involving his favourite fish, smoked haddock, so the chefs came up with the omelette which pleased Bennett so much that he ordered it everywhere he went. He must have eaten a lot of eggs as he personally spread the fame of the omelette that bore his name.

OYSTERS ROCKEFELLER

Oysters in their shell with a topping, usually of a rich butter sauce, are named after John Davison Rockefeller I (1839–1937). The name was a sly dig at Rockefeller, who was America's richest man when the dish was invented at the famous Antoine's Restaurant in New Orleans in 1899. The creator of the original dish, Jules Alciatore, passed the recipe only to his successors, and in Antoine's to this day they will tell you that all other restaurants serve a pale imitation. Rockefeller was possibly not best pleased at such a rich dish being named after him, as he never touched alcohol or tobacco and was a Baptist who firmly believed in 'nothing to excess' – except for wealth, most of which he gave away. The Rockefellers may also suffer from a lack of imagination – current Senator John Davison 'Jay' Rockefeller is the fourth generation to bear exactly the same name, and his son is called John Davison, too.

PAVLOVA

Australians and New Zealanders can be combustible when mixed, so, if you are ever in a group consisting of people from these two fine nations, don't mention Pavlova. Named in honour of the legendary Russian ballet dancer Anna Pavlova (1881–1931), there has been a long-running argument as to whether the concoction of meringue, cream and fruit was invented in Wellington, New Zealand, in 1926 when she visited the city, or in the Esplanade Hotel in Perth, Australia, in 1935, Pavlova having stayed there in 1929. It really does cause arguments between the two countries, but, given that a dish called 'Pavlova' was mentioned in a New Zealand cookbook in 1927, the evidence does point in their favour.

PEACH MELBA

Another dish named in honor of Dame Nellie Melba (see *Melba Toast* above).

PICKLES

The practice of pickling fish, as we in the West understand it, was started in the 14th century by Dutch fisherman Willem Beukelz. The name was mispronounced by English traders, and 'pickles' soon spread to Britain and elsewhere. Then other foods were pickled to preserve them before a 'pickle', such as dill pickle, was created.

PIZZA MARGHERITA

With its colours of the Italian flag – white from mozzarella cheese, red from tomatoes and green from basil – this dish was named by Italian public acclaim in honour of Queen Margherita of Savoy (1851–1926), queen consort to King Umberto I of Italy, after she visited Naples and was served a slice of the pizza.

POMMES ANNA

Sliced potatoes cooked in butter, the dish is usually said to have been invented by French chef Adolphe Dugléré, the head chef at the Café Anglais who cooked the famous Dinner of the Three Emperors at the restaurant in 1867, and after whom the recipe for Sole à la Dugléré is named. Though this derivation is disputed, it seems likely the chef called his potato dish after Anna Deslions, a high-class courtesan who rejoiced in the nickname of the Lioness of the Boulevards and who was the guest of many a gentleman at the Café Anglais.

PRALINE

Pralines differ in recipe from country to country but generally they consist of crushed nuts in chocolate or syrup confections. Again, this is another example of the inventor being ignored in favour of his aristocratic employer, for the 'praline' in question was César, duc de Choiseul, comte du Plessis-Praslin (1598–1675), the Marshal of France, whose cook dreamed up the first powdered nut sweet.

QUEEN MOTHER'S CAKE

The Queen Mother, the late and much-lamented Elizabeth Bowes Lyon (1900–2002), queen consort of King George VI and mother of Britain's present monarch, was fond of this date and walnut confection. She gave out the recipe on condition that it was only to be used by cakemakers raising money for charity with their home baking. The Queen Mother evidently loved cakes of all kind, so much so that her nickname among family and friends was 'Cake'.

RUMFORD SOUP

Sir Benjamin Thompson, Count Rumford (1753–1814), was the forerunner of today's nutritionist chefs. Born in Massachusetts while it was still part of Britain, when the American War of Independence broke out, he sided with the old country. He moved to England, where he became a government minister and was knighted, and where he started inventing things such as a new, efficient chimney which made him famous and wealthy.

In 1785, he moved to Bavaria in modern-day Germany and, always interested in scientific experiments, he proceeded to invent yet more useful items, such as a coffee percolator, as well as doing research on the nature of heat and cold.

Impressed by his studies on everything from candles to food, the Bavarian Government asked him to come up with a way of feeding the poor in workhouses. Mixing barley, dried peas, potato, salt and old sour beer, Rumford created the soup that bears his name, and it was such a success that Rumford's Soup was fed to prisoners into the 20th century.

SACHERTORTE

How could anyone fight a legal battle over decades about a piece of chocolate cake? Yet that is exactly what happened to the Sacher family of Vienna, Austria, from 1930 through to the 1960s. Even its origins were sensational – in 1832, Prince Klemens von Metternich was holding a special dinner for titled guests when his head chef became ill. Franz Sacher (1816–1907) was the apprentice in the kitchen, and he hurriedly devised a chocolate cake with apricot jam in the middle and chocolate icing. Needless to say, the Prince's reputation as a host was saved, and the young chef's reputation was made.

His son Eduard opened a Hotel Sacher in Vienna and, with the recipe a jealously guarded secret, the hotel flourished as the sole retailer of the 'original Sacher Torte'. But in the 1930s depression, the hotel went bust and Eduard

Junior, Franz's grandson, had to go and work for Demel's Bakery in the city, taking 'Eduard Sacher Torte' with him.

When the Hotel Sacher reopened in 1938 under new management, it claimed to have the 'Original', and, while the argument went quiet during the Second World War, in 1954, Demel went to court saying it had the rights to the original. The main difference was whether the torte had one layer of jam or two. It took lots of court time and depositions by witnesses before an out-of-court settlement was agreed, and both versions of the cake are still sold with the hotel having the rights to the 'Original' name.

To this day, 'Original Sachertorte' can only be made in Vienna and Salzburg, and Bolzano in Italy, while Demel's is rated better by many experts. All other 'Sacher' tortes are imitations.

SALADE OLIVIER

If Lucien Olivier (1838–83) was alive today, he would barely recognise the salad which he invented and which bears his name. In his Hermitage restaurant in Moscow in the 1860s, Olivier, who was of Belgian extraction, served up a salad of grouse, smoked duck, caviar, veal tongue, lettuce, capers and seafood plus other ingredients depending on the season. The dressing was his own concoction and he kept it secret until his death. Now known in many countries as 'Russian Salad', the modern version is very inferior, due no doubt to the rarity and significant cost of the ingredients. Everything from boiled potatoes to peas and mayonnaise – obviously no one knows what was in his dressing – goes into a modern 'Salade

Olivier', but Russians in particular cling to the salad as a holiday feast dish, even if Lucien would not approve.

SANDWICH

Among the world's most used eponyms on a daily basis, the sandwich takes its name from the 4th Earl of Sandwich, John Montagu (1718–92), who had his servants bring him a meal of cuts of meat between slices of bread to sustain him during long sessions at his desk or the gambling tables. His friends began to ask for similar snacks 'like a Sandwich' and thus began a global love affair with bread and fillings.

Edward Gibbon, best known for writing *The Decline and Fall of the Roman Empire*, mentioned eating 'a Sandwich' in his journal, proving that the term was already in current usage in the late 18th century and giving strong evidence that the derivation is correct.

The Earl of Sandwich was at one time the First Lord of the Admiralty and his protégé Captain James Cook named the Sandwich Islands after him. We know these islands better as the State of Hawaii, a name which means 'Place of the Gods'. No doubt President Barack Obama prefers that his birthplace be a 'place of the Gods' rather than 'two slices of bread with cheese and ham, please'.

SHIRLEY TEMPLE COCKTAIL

She was the greatest child star of them all, yet, like every other child in the USA in the 1930s, Shirley Temple was not allowed to drink alcohol, even though she had to attend premières and parties like any other big star.

A friendly bartender in Los Angeles is supposed to have

mixed her a drink that looked like a cocktail, consisting of orange juice, ginger ale and grenadine. Many people have claimed they invented the drink, but there was only one Shirley Temple (b. 1928), the girl from Santa Monica in California who was the most popular star of the 1930s. She made a string of hit movies before quitting to attend high school at the age of 12. Temple made a brief comeback but abandoned movies altogether at the age of 22, by which time she had already married and divorced actor James Agar. She later met the wealthy former naval officer Charles Alden Black, and they were married for almost 55 years until his death in 2005.

After a stint on television in the 1950s and '60s, Shirley Temple Black took up politics as a Republican, and later served as ambassador to Ghana and Czechoslovakia under Presidents Richard Nixon and Gerald Ford respectively. She lives in Northern California, and is reckoned to be the last surviving major star of pre-war films.

STRAWBERRIES ROMANOFF

There are three distinct versions of this dish – Russian, French and American – with only strawberries and some form of liqueur as constants. Not surprisingly, there are also several versions of how it got its name. The best known is that 'Prince' Michael Romanoff, real name Hershel Geguzin, made some 'improvements' to the existing French version at his famous 1940s Hollywood restaurant and called it after himself in a typically flamboyant manner.

STROGANOFF

Beef (or other meat or vegetables) Stroganoff is a Russian dish mixing pieces of beef with mushrooms and sour cream which was first mentioned in a cookbook in the middle of the 19th century when the powerful Stroganov family was at its zenith. There is no claim that the Stroganovs, who were descended from peasants but became hugely rich merchants and politicians, invented the dish, but it was most certainly served in their household. Perhaps Count Sergei Grigoriyevich Stroganov (1794–1882), the Governor of Moscow, has the best claim to be the man whose name adorns the recipe.

TARTE TATIN

Another accidental creation, this time by Stéphanie Tatin (1838–1917) when she was hard at work in the kitchen of the Hotel Tatin which she ran with her sister Caroline (1847–1911). The small hotel in Lamotte-Beuvron in Sologne in France was renowned locally for, among other things, the apple pies cooked by Stéphanie. Overly busy one day, she prepared her apples in sauté butter and sugar, the mixture which gave her pie its delicious caramelised taste. On this occasion, she forgot to line the dish with pastry, but decided that the mixture would cook just as well if she laid the pastry on top.

When she removed the upside-down pie and inverted it, the topless tart looked and tasted *superbe*, as they say in France, and a great new recipe was born.

TETRAZZINI

As with a lot of recipes, there are competing claims for the originator. This dish, made with either turkey, chicken or seafood, may have occurred in the Palace Hotel in San Francisco or the Knickerbocker Hotel in New York, but there is absolutely no doubt that the dish was named in honour of Luisa Tetrazzini (1871–1940), the Italian soprano whose fame was at its height when the dish first appeared around 1909. SanFran has the better claim as Luisa lived there for years. Interestingly, Luisa's greatest stage competitor was Nellie Melba (see *Melba Toast* and *Peach Melba* above).

TOOTSIE POP

Not much seen in Britain, more's the pity, Tootsie Pops, like Tootsie Rolls, are sweets – candy in American parlance – which get their name from Clara Hirshfield, daughter of Leo Hirshfield, an immigrant from Austria who invented the Tootsie Roll in New York in the last years of the 19th century. Clara was nicknamed 'Tootsie', and her proud dad called his new sweet after her. It became wildly popular, and Tootsie Pops – the world's best-selling lollipop – followed years later so that Tootsie Roll Industries is now one of the biggest manufacturers of sweets in the world.

TOURNEDOS ROSSINI

Named in honour of the Italian composer of the operas *The Barber of Seville* and *William Tell* with its famous overture.

It is not certain which French chef created the dish, as

Auguste Escoffier and Cassimir Moison are both credited with its invention. The latter probably has the best claim as he was a friend of Gioachino Antonio Rossini (1792–1868) during the composer's years in Paris where the dish originated.

VICTORIA SPONGE

Like hundreds of towns and streets and a lake and waterfall in Africa, this sponge is named in honour of Queen Victoria.

VEUVE CLICQUOT

The name in French means the 'widow Clicquot' and, sadly for the poor lady, she was indeed bereft of a husband. Madame Barbe-Nicole Clicquot (1777–1866) was the daughter-in-law of Philippe Clicquot-Muiron who founded the famous champagne house in 1772. Madame inherited the management of the company when her husband of just over six years, Francis Clicquot, died in mysterious circumstances in 1805.

The daughter of a Count, Nicholas Ponsardin, Madame Clicquot was not typical of women of the age, in that she was both well educated and a formidable businesswoman in her own right. She was also well connected, as the Emperor Napoleon knew and favoured her family.

Madame Clicquot used those impeccable connections well as she spread the news of her champagne across the courts of Europe, and what the monarchs drank, people wanted to swallow by the gallon.

More crucial for the history of champagne, Madame Clicquot was instrumental in developing the process of '*remuage*' or 'riddling' – a way of removing yeast from bottles – using a special rack. This system dramatically improved the wine and enabled much greater production, thus bringing about champagne as we know it. With a superb wine, and a driving force such as the Madame, the house of Clicquot Ponsardin became the foremost champagne company in the world by the middle of the 19th century and, in tribute to its founder, Veuve Clicquot became the standard name of its best product.

WASHINGTON PIE

This cake-pie is not named after the State or President George, but after Martha Washington (1731–1802), George's wife and the first First Lady of the USA. Martha was a wealthy widower when she married George Washington. She bravely followed her husband on his campaigns, and then ran his household during his Presidency, calling on the *Booke of Cookery* that she kept from a young age, and which was later published. The recipe for the eponymous pie is in the book.

WOOLTON PIE

Frederick Marquis, the 1st Lord Woolton, was Britain's Minister of Food during the Second World War, and his name became attached to a pie which, most unusually for the British, contained no meat.

The recipe was created by master chef Francis Latry of the Savoy Hotel in one of numerous attempts to get the public to eat vegetables rather than meat, which was rationed. Lord Woolton was an enthusiastic proponent of the pie, and his name stuck to it. It fell out of favour as soon as rationing ended, but has enjoyed renewed popularity among vegetarians in recent years.

·8·

NAME, SET AND MATCH

ALI SHUFFLE

Muhammad Ali (b. 1942), best known as 'The Greatest', excited hatred and admiration in equal quantities when he first burst on the world sporting scene in the 1960s. At first, as Cassius Marcellus Clay, he was an American hero, winning gold in the light-heavyweight division of the 1960 Olympic Games in Rome. Later, as world heavyweight champion, he was the most athletic boxer of that weight in history, while his fast-talking wit soon earned him the nickname of the 'Louisville Lip'.

His change of religion to Islam, and his backing of a militant campaign for black civil rights as well as his principled opposition to being drafted into the Vietnam War, earned him the enmity of much of white America, yet he overcame all the opposition to be treasured as a man of peace whose personal odyssey is one of the greatest stories of the 20th century.

His dazzling boxing skills included the famous Ali

Shuffle, a lightning-quick skipping adjustment of his feet that bamboozled his opponents. It was really just a bit of showboating, but it helped Ali focus and retain his rhythm as he prepared to deliver a hammer blow to his opponents who were usually mesmerised by the dancing feet.

Here's the knockout – it may well be called the Ali Shuffle, but The Greatest did not invent the idea of a quick hop and skip to change the leading foot and throw your opponents off guard. Credit for that must go to one of his predecessors as world heavyweight champion, Jersey Joe Walcott (1914–94), real name Arnold Raymond Cream.

Called the Walcott Shift, the move involved Jersey Joe switching from leading with his left foot forward to his right, or vice versa, in the blink of an eye, and Ali saw this on film and copied it, according to his trainer Angelo Dundee. The Greatest added his own dazzling speed to make it the Ali Shuffle, and it became such an iconic move in sport that there have even been pop songs with the eponym in the title or lyrics.

Though Jersey Joe Walcott was a terrific fighter, neither he nor any other heavyweight could ever have hoped to emulate The Greatest, Muhammad Ali, so the Shuffle is credited to the man from Louisville.

Yet, if everyone had kept their real name and the move was properly attributed, the Ali Shuffle would be known as the Cream Shift.

Ali is not in good health these days, but let us hope it is many years before he shuffles off his mortal coil.

AXEL

One of the oldest eponyms in sport, the Axel jump in ice skating was first displayed in public in 1882 by Axel Paulsen (1855–1938), although it is likely that the Norwegian, who won that year's event, had been demonstrating his innovative jump in private for months or years beforehand.

Paulsen was better known as a speed skater at a time when that form of the sport enjoyed greater prestige and prize money than 'fancy', i.e. figure, skating.

At what is now considered to have been the first major international skating championships in Vienna in 1882, Axel stunned the public by skating backwards and then rotating to go forward on his speed skates and then going into a jump off the outside edge of his skate, completing a rotation-and-a-half in the air and landing going backwards. The Axel is still the only recognised jump in figure skating where the take-off happens going forward.

Axel's domination of the sport in the 1880s – he was recognised as the world's best speed skater for eight consecutive years – meant that everyone copied his moves, and soon male skaters in particular vied to introduce variations on the Axel. It took more than 60 years for a full Double Axel to be landed, and not until the 1987 World Figure Skating Championships did Brian Orser of Canada land the first Triple Axel in competition.

No one has yet landed a Quadruple Axel successfully in competition, while only four women have ever managed a Triple Axel, with film star Sonja Henie (1912–69) being credited as the first woman to perform an Axel.

BOSMAN

Doing or signing a Bosman is a term from football. It refers to Jean-Marc Bosman (b. 1964), a little-known Belgian player who challenged the way European football was run as it was full of restrictive practices that made players virtual slaves. It took him five years to battle through the courts, but eventually in 1995 the European Court of Justice ruled that Bosman and all other players were entitled to freedom of movement within the European Union after their contracts were finished. The result was that players and their agents became much more powerful. Bosman lost his career, but every highly paid footballer in Europe owes him their wealth.

Some people in football, especially club chairmen and owners, wish Bosman had never come along. But then they also usually believe that footballers are chattels and should not be subject to basic human rights.

BOSIE

Another name for a googly. In cricket, a ball that is bowled by a right-handed spin bowler which breaks in a different direction from its apparent path is said to be a 'wrong 'un' or googly, while such a ball delivered by a left-hander is known as a 'chinaman googly'.

It is still sometimes called a 'bosie' after English cricketer Bernard Bosanquet (1877–1936) who invented it in the early 1900s. Bosanquet played seven times for England, taking 25 wickets for his country. His son Reginald (1932–84) was the famous newsreader for ITN.

BUSBY BABES

One of the greatest teams in the history of football, the Manchester United side of the mid- to late 1950s were young and gifted and threatened to dominate English and European football for a decade after winning the English League in 1955/56 and 1956/57. Yet, on a snowy night at Munich Airport in February 1958, most of the side were killed or seriously injured in an aircraft which crashed off the end of the runway in bad weather. For those of a certain age, or any Man United fan, the names of the dead conjure up an image of past glory that can never fade, as they were taken so cruelly and prematurely.

Players Geoff Bent, Roger Byrne, Eddie Colman, Duncan Edwards, David Begg, Tommy Taylor and Billy 'Liam' Whelan were all killed, while Jackie Blanchflower and Johnny Berry were too badly injured to play again. Two crew members, three United staff, eight journalists, a travel agent and a supporter were also killed.

The Babes get their name from one of the survivors of that crash, Sir Matt Busby (1909–94), the first of a breed of manager who transformed the way professional football operates. The son of a Lanarkshire miner, Busby grew up to become a useful footballer who played, somewhat ironically, for United's great rivals Manchester City and Liverpool. He was capped once for Scotland.

It was after he was asked to coach United, however, that he found his role in life – to build a super team and a club that would eventually become the biggest in the world.

Busby brought a new and highly professional approach to management. Before him, hardly any team was coached in skills and tactics, but, influenced by the great Hungarian sides of the 1950s, Busby and other managers such as Sir Alf Ramsay, Tommy Docherty, Bill Shankly and Jock Stein preached fitness, skill and tactical awareness to their men. Deep psychological understanding and man management was his forte. In short, Busby and his cohorts invented modern football management.

Despite nearly dying at Munich, Busby survived to lead a rebuilt United, with Denis Law, Bobby Charlton, Nobby Stiles and George Best as the backbone, to the European Cup in 1968. He remains revered as the founding father of modern United, and as the man who gave his name to a fabulous but doomed team.

COMANECI SALTO

Nadia Comaneci of Romania (b. 1961) gave arguably the greatest display ever by a woman gymnast at the Olympic Games in Montreal in 1976 when, at the age of 15, she won three gold medals, a silver and a bronze, compiling seven perfect ten scores along the way – the first gymnast ever to gain a ten at the Olympics. She won two more golds and two silvers at the Moscow Olympics in 1980.

Her variation on the salto – the gymnastic term for a somersault – was performed on the asymmetric or uneven bars and involved her somersaulting from the high bar and catching hold of the bar again. It is still classed as one of the most difficult of all gymnastic manoeuvres and very few women attempt it.

Comaneci became a coach and administrator and married American gymnast Bart Conner. She is now an honorary consul in the USA for the Romanian Government and is the only woman to have twice been awarded the Olympic Order by the International Olympic Committee.

CRUYFF TURN

The greatest Dutch footballer of them all and one of the most skilful players ever, Johan Cruyff (b. 1947) perfected the dribbling move which bears his name, a swift turn and drag of the ball that leaves opponents tackling thin air. He showed it to best effect in the 1974 World Cup when the Netherlands played Sweden and Cruyff did the turn, leaving Swedish defender Jan Olsson in his wake – it's on YouTube if you want to view it. Now every player who fancies himself as skilful has the Cruyff Turn in his armoury – but nobody does it like the master.

DERBY

If a coin had fallen the other way, the world's most famous races on the flat, and sport's many great local contests, would now be called 'Bunburies'. The 'local derby' in football would be called the 'local bunbury', while the 'bunbury hat' would be what an American calls a bowler hat. The Brown Derby just would not exist under that name of bunbury.

Really, no offence to that lovely parish in Cheshire, but 'derby' just sounds and reads better than 'bunbury'. Yet it was so close.

Sir Charles Bunbury, 6th baronet of that name, loved horse racing and, in 1779, when his friend Edward Smith-Stanley, the 12th Earl of Derby (1752–1834), proposed a colts' race over land near Epsom, Bunbury was the first to support him.

That year, Lord Derby had organised a fillies' race over a mile in and around Epsom, which he named after his Surrey residence, The Oaks. It remains the oldest Classic race for fillies in the world.

At the dinner table after the Oaks, Lord Derby and Sir Charles Bunbury and all the aristocracy present agreed to toss a coin to see if the new colts' race should take the name of their host or Sir Charles, and the coin fell in Lord Derby's favour.

The race was duly run in 1780, and Bunbury became its first winner with the legendary Diomed.

Bunbury's luck seems to have been variable. He may have won that first Derby, but he married the beautiful and wilful Lady Sarah Lennox, daughter of the second Duke of Richmond, only for her to leave him for Lord William Gordon, the father of her daughter Louisa. Despite Louisa's parentage being uncontested – she was her daddy's spitting image – Bunbury still had to petition Parliament for a divorce, as was the law in those days, and it cost him a small fortune to end his marriage through this Act of Parliament. His second marriage, to Lady Margaret, was childless and nowadays only the Bunbury Handicap at Newmarket and the Diomed Stakes at Epsom commemorate him.

Lord Derby's name, however, is ubiquitous, and it is all thanks to the horse race which for more than two centuries has been the Blue Riband of the sport. Local derbies were so named because, in the early days of organised professional sport in Victorian-era Britain, commentators really had only one event to which they could compare exciting and well-attended matches – the Epsom Derby, the biggest event in British and indeed world sport in terms of crowds and interest.

The Kentucky Derby, with its interesting pronunciation, and all other racing derbies take their name from the original and, in the USA, bowler hats became known as 'derbies' because they were the sort of headgear people wore to attend or take part in big race meetings.

FOSBURY FLOP

There were many extraordinary scenes in the Olympic Games of 1968. Apart from the Black Power salutes given by the American medallists Tommie Smith and John Carlos which saw them suspended from the Games, gymnast Vera Caslavska won four gold medals for Czechoslovakia and was then banned from international competition for refusing to acknowledge the Soviet anthem. Drug tests were introduced at the Games, and it is often forgotten that these Games saw the arrival of East Germany as a separate Olympic nation after years of protest. And that was just the political controversy.

Bob Beamon obliterated the long jump world record amid extraordinary scenes, while discus champion Al Oerter of the USA became the first competitor to win four consecutive gold medals in a track and field event. Then there was the men's high jump.

Watching on colour television for the first time, many people across the world simply could not believe their eyes when Richard 'Dick' Fosbury (b. 1947), a tall, slim young American, ran in a J shape towards the take-off area and then reversed so that he flew backwards up and over the bar, arching his back and kicking out his legs to clear the bar. It was an extraordinary thing to see, going against all the 'run forward and leap' thinking. It was simply one of the most revolutionary techniques ever seen in any track and field sport.

Back home in the USA, people had openly laughed when they first saw Fosbury's jumping style, so completely different from the straddle jump that was in vogue, and only possible because foam rubber mattresses had been brought in to give jumpers a softer landing.

A journalist wrote that he looked like a fish flopping on a boat ... and the Fosbury Flop was born. They all stopped laughing when Fosbury won the Olympic trials in the USA, and the world applauded with excitement and raved about his ingenuity when the Flop took him to the Olympic gold medal in Mexico City.

Fosbury, who never took a dime for his athletics, revolutionised high jumping and nearly all the top competitors nowadays are 'Floppers'. The man himself became a successful engineer and businessman, beat off a bout of cancer, and is now President of the World Olympians Association, representing the 80,000 people who have competed at the Olympic Games. Very few of them, however, caused quite such a sensation as Dick Fosbury and his eponymous Flop.

HAIL MARY PASS

Originating in American football and now used in several sports, this 'desperation' pass is named after Mary, the mother of Jesus Christ and refers to the best-known prayer to her, the Hail Mary, or Ave Maria in Latin. It was first used to refer to a last-minute, seemingly last-ditch pass following the Dallas Cowboys v Minnesota Vikings play-off match in December 1975, when Cowboys' quarterback Roger Staubach from a hopeless position threw a 50-yard winning touchdown pass to Drew Pearson to defeat the Minnesota Vikings 17–14 with seconds remaining.

Joking with the press afterwards, Staubach, who had been raised a Catholic, said that, when he threw his sensational pass, he closed his eyes 'and said a Hail Mary'. The name stuck in the popular imagination.

HARVEY SMITH 'V' SIGN

Winston Churchill should have copyrighted his famous 'V' for victory gesture. Instead, showjumper Harvey Smith (b. 1938) made the rude, palm-inwards version – equivalent to flipping the finger in the USA – his own with a very public, televised example of the sign in 1971.

Smith, a rebellious Yorkshireman who was a huge hit with the public but not the stuffy authorities of showjumping, had just won the Showjumping Derby at Hickstead for the second time when he gave the two-fingered salute to the judges. They stripped him of his title and confiscated his £2,000 prize, but had to reinstate him as winner a few days later after a huge public outcry and Smith's defence that it was a 'victory' sign, just like Churchill. He later admitted he really meant it to be insulting.

HASKELL

In golf, for many years the ball was known as a 'Haskell'

after Coburn Haskell (1868–1922) who invented the rubber-cored, rubber-filament wrapped ball along with his colleague Bertram G Work. After the new ball was shown to add 20 yards to the average golfer's drive, the old gutta percha (latex-like) balls became obsolete overnight and Haskells swept the world, making the inventor very rich.

Another Haskell, the computer programming language, is named after Haskell Curry (1900–82), the American logician and mathematician who also has the Curry language and the computing term 'currying' named after him.

HENMAN HILL

The most famous hill in British sport is actually called Aorangi Terrace. It rises alongside Number One Court at Wimbledon, where spectators gather to watch the action on a giant television screen. It is named after Tim Henman (b. 1974), the former British number one who never won Wimbledon but who united the country as he tried his heart out in the tournament.

HOBDAY

An operation to cure breathing difficulties in horses, it is not performed nearly as frequently today as it used to be, due to improvements in treatment. It is named after veterinary surgeon Sir Frederick Hobday (1869–1939) who devised the technique.

KORBUT FLIP

There are two skills in gymnastics named after Olga Korbut (b. 1955), the Olympic champion born in Belarus when it was part of the Soviet Union. She was the first gymnast to perform the eponymous flips, most notably at the Olympic Games in Munich in 1972 when she captivated the world with her daring and enchanting routines. Both are somersaults, one performed on the balance beam and one on the uneven bars. The latter is now banned because it involved standing on the higher bar which the gymnastic authorities consider too dangerous.

LONSDALE BELT

The most famous belt in sport is named after the man who introduced it to the sport of boxing. Hugh Lowther, 5th Earl of Lonsdale (1857–1944), first President of the Automobile Association, loved his sport, and was first President of the National Sporting Club in London as well as master of hounds and chairman of Arsenal FC.

At the National Sporting Club, which made professional boxing a reputable sport in Britain, Lord Lonsdale donated a belt that incorporated porcelain and 22-carat gold to be awarded to the holder of the British championship in each weight division. If a boxer defended his title twice, he was allowed to keep the belt. The British Boxing Board of Control took over the running of the sport and has awarded the highly prized belts since 1936. Noted outright winners include Bombardier Billy Wells, Lennox Lewis and Henry Cooper, the only man to win three Lonsdale belts outright.

MARADONA MOVE

The ability to dribble a football, spin 360 degrees, baffle your opponents and carry on going with the ball at your feet is given to few footballers. Diego Armando Maradona (b. 1960), the greatest Argentinean footballer of all time, practised the art of dribbling ceaselessly, and incorporated spinning into his movement. He first showed the full spin move as a teenager, and then used it in World Cup matches. Zinedine Zidane (b. 1972) copied the move and perfected it, and, when the Frenchman did the spin, it was called the roulette.

MULLIGAN

This eponym started in golf and is now used in a variety of sports, card and video games and, indeed, in life in general. It means retaking a shot without penalty because you have duffed the first one and, crucially, being given the second chance to do so by your opponents.

It is not something one should try in the Open Championship, or even when competing for local club honours, but among friends making an early-morning start to their round, a mulligan is perfectly acceptable, but only on the first tee, or, at best, one each per nine holes out and in. Any more just wouldn't be cricket … or even golf.

There are several claims to be the Mulligan who started this 'get out' clause in golf. The best evidence seems to be that John A Mulligan, known to everyone as Buddy, was a locker-room attendant at Essex Falls Country Club in New Jersey and occasionally got to play a round with members.

One day he was playing with assistant professional David O'Connell and local journalist Des Sullivan. Mulligan hit a poor shot off the first tee and begged his playing partners for another chance, as he had been working and they had been practising. Sullivan and O'Connell graciously conceded, and Mulligan duly spread the story so that club members began allowing 'mulligans' as Buddy had done. After being made golfing editor on the local *Newark Evening News*, Sullivan began to use 'mulligans' in his column, and the name caught on from there.

Significantly, there is no written record of the eponym before the 1930s when Sullivan started to write about mulligans. There is some evidence, however, that the Mulligan in question might have been David of the clan, who was playing at the Country Club of Montreal when he played what he called a 'correction shot'. He apparently repeated the stunt at the Winged Foot Club in New York which he joined in 1937 and, in later years, he would happily claim credit for inventing the mulligan.

QUEENSBERRY RULES

Scottish nobleman John Graham, 9th Marquess of Queensberry (1844–1900), did not write the rules of boxing, which still guide the sport to this day. Instead, it was John Graham Chambers (1843–83) who published the new code in 1867. Chambers' ideas on three-minute rounds, mandatory gloves, a ten-second count and no wrestling impressed the Marquess who agreed to allow his name to be attached to them. Both men were keen sportsmen, Queensberry helping to found the Amateur Athletic Association, and being a keen hunter and racehorse owner. Chambers rowed for Cambridge in the Boat Race, and staged championship events in a whole host of sports.

Queensberry may have endorsed the 'fair fight' rules

because, as an atheist, he was used to unfair treatment in society. But his rules on fair play did not extend to the playwright Oscar Wilde, whom he infamously hounded into jail, bankruptcy and exile over his affair with Queensberry's son, Lord Alfred Douglas.

SALCHOW

Possibly the best-known eponymous ice-skating jump, the Salchow is named after the man who invented it, Karl Emil Julius Ulrich Salchow (1877–1949). Born in Denmark but of Swedish nationality, Salchow won the world figure skating championships ten times and was Olympic champion in 1908 when figure skating was part of the summer Games in London.

He first used the jump, which involves swinging one leg to gain momentum for a take-off on the edge of the other skate, in 1909. Double, triple and even quadruple Salchows have been performed in competition in the decades since then.

TSUKAHARA

In gymnastics, a full twisting double salto (somersault) in the tuck position either as part of a tumble routine or a dismount from apparatus is known as a 'Tsukahara' after the Japanese gymnast who first performed it.

Mitsuo Tsukahara (b. 1947) won five Olympic Gold medals and was a vital member of the Japanese men's team which swept all before it in the late 1960s and early 1970s.

He also has the Tsukahara vault, another type of salto performed on the horse or table, named after him as the first man to achieve it in competition.

VARDON GRIP

The most common way of gripping a golf club is the interlocking hold known as the Vardon Grip after Harry Vardon (1870–1930) from Jersey in the Channel Islands who popularised it when he became the world's most famous golfer, winning the Open Championship a record six times and also the US Open of 1900. At one point, he won 14 tournaments in a row, also still a record.

Yet Vardon did not invent the eponymous grip. The first man to play regularly with the grip, in which the little finger of the bottom hand on the club is locked on to the club by the forefinger of the top hand, was Johnny Laidlay (1860–1940), a Scottish golfer from East Lothian, who won the British Amateur Championship twice and finished runner-up as an amateur in the Open Championship of 1893. He never turned professional, or else the Vardon Grip might well be known as the Laidlay Grip.

EPONYMOUS LISTS

MONTHS
The eight eponymous months

JANUARY
In Roman belief, Janus or Ianuarius was the god of change and new beginnings as well as gates and doors. He is invariably depicted with two faces, which is why an untrustworthy or hypocritical person is often called a Janus.

FEBRUARY
A rare case of an inverted eponym. Named by the Romans after the festival of spring cleaning called Februa, a god was later devised to personify the month and festival, and he was called Februus.

MARCH
The month of Mars, Roman god of war.

APRIL

Named after Aphrodite, Greek goddess of beauty and love, equivalent to the Roman goddess Venus.

MAY

The month of Maia, Greek goddess of fertility.

JUNE

From the Roman goddess Juno, wife of Jupiter. She was Hera to the Greeks.

JULY

Named after Julius Caesar by the Emperor Augustus. Julius Caesar reorganised the Roman calendar and called the month Quintilis as it was the fifth month.

AUGUST

When Augustus became Emperor, he renamed Quintilis in honour of his uncle Julius, and then called the sixth month Sextilis, after himself. Modest chap.

DAYS

The five eponymous days:

TUESDAY

Named after Tiw or Tyr, the Norse and early German pagan god of war. The concept of a day named after a war god originated with the Romans, and Tuesday is still 'Mars' day in Latin-based languages.

WEDNESDAY

The day of Woden, the Old English name of Wotan, or Odin in Norse mythology, the king of their gods in Valhalla.

THURSDAY

Thor's day, named after the Norse god of thunder.

FRIDAY

The day of Freyja, the Norse goddess of love.

SATURDAY

Named after the planet Saturn, which in turn was named after the Roman god of agriculture and the Golden Age of peace.

CONSTELLATIONS

The following ten constellations take their name from figures in Greek mythology:

ANDROMEDA

She was the daughter of Cassiopeia, a queen who boasted that she was more beautiful than the goddess Hera and the nymphs. Poseidon, god of the sea, decided to send a sea monster to ruin Cassiopeia's country, and the only way to placate him was to offer the virginal Andromeda as a sacrifice. The hero Perseus rescued Andromeda and took her in marriage.

CASSIOPEIA

In the Greek astronomer Ptolemy's list of constellations, the proud mother of Andromeda is commemorated in the name.

CEPHEUS
Ptolemy called this constellation after the fabled King of Ethiopia.

HERCULES
Greek form of Heracles, and another of Ptolemy's names.

HYDRA
Named by Ptolemy after the multi-headed monster, slain by Hercules.

ORION
One of the most prominent of all constellations with its belt of three stars, Orion was the first great hunter.

PEGASUS
Named by Ptolemy after the winged horse of the gods.

PERSEUS
He slew Medusa the Gorgon, rescued Andromeda and was an all-round good guy who founded the kingdom of Mycenae. There is evidence that such a king existed, and myths and legends grew up around him.

PLEIADES
The seven sisters of Greek mythology were the daughters of Atlas and were all very naughty girls, having affairs with several gods.

SAGITTARIUS
The half-man, half-horse centaur whose skill with a bow and arrow is immortalised in a constellation and zodiac sign.

COMETS
A dozen eponymous comets

AREND ROLAND
Discovered in 1956 by Sylvain Arend and Georges Roland of Belgium. They spotted it on photographic plates.

BENNETT
First seen in 1969 by John Caister 'Jack' Bennett (1914–90) of South Africa, a successful comet hunter who was an amateur astronomer.

CAESAR
Known as the Great Comet, it appeared in the sky shortly after the assassination of Julius Caesar in 44BC. Visible during the day because it was so bright, the Romans took it as a sign that Caesar had become a god.

HALE-BOPP
Found independently and simultaneously in 1995 by two Americans, astronomer Alan Hale (b. 1958), and Thomas Bopp (b. 1959), an amateur astronomer who was using a borrowed telescope.

HALLEY'S
The best-known example of an eponym which does not

recognise the actual discoverer (see *Stigler's Law*, chapter 5). Edmond Halley (1656–1742) merely worked out the periodicity of the comet – it is visible from Earth every 75–76 years – which had been observed and charted since ancient times.

Halley's name could have been applied to several things – he discovered hundreds of stars, strongly influenced the development of actuarial science, invented a diving bell he used in the River Thames, and worked out a way of predicting the path of an eclipse. Ironically, the latter achievement made him world famous at the time, not the comet for which he is best remembered now.

IKEYA-SEKI

The sensation of 1965, this comet was so bright it could be seen in daytime. It also broke into three pieces as it approached its point nearest the sun. Its finders were Kaoru Ikeya (b. 1943) of Japan, who has found four comets in all, and Tsutomo Seki (b. 1930), director of the Geisei Observatory in Japan, and famed as a comet hunter who has discovered more than 200 of them as well as a number of asteroids.

KOHOUTEK

One of several comets named after Czech astronomer Lubos Kohoutek (b. 1935). This comet appeared in 1973 and, though visible to the naked eye, it never lived up to the brightness predicted for it.

MISS MITCHELL

Originally credited to Italian astronomer Francesco de Vico

(1805–48), who was then given one of the King of Denmark's medals for being the first person to discover a comet using a telescope.

Over in America, however, Miss Maria Mitchell (1818–89), a Quaker teacher and librarian from Nantucket in Massachusetts, had actually discovered the comet two days earlier than De Vico. Miss Mitchell got her medal, and later became the first female professional astronomer in the USA.

SHOEMAKER-LEVY 9

Remembered for the extraordinary images produced when it broke up and collided with Jupiter, this comet was named after its collaborating discoverers, the Americans Eugene Shoemaker (1928–97) and his wife Carolyn (b. 1929) and Canadian Richard Levy (b. 1948). It was one of a number of comets discovered by the trio, but was unique both in its destruction and the fact that it orbited Jupiter rather than the Sun.

SWIFT-TUTTLE

Found independently in 1862 by American astronomers Lewis Swift (1820–1913) and Horace Parnell Tuttle (1837–1923), when it swept by Earth in 1992 it was calculated that this comet has the potential to strike Earth in a few thousand years' time. It gives us the Perseid meteor shower.

THATCHER

No, not her … found in 1861 by Professor AE Thatcher of New York, this comet is responsible for the annual Lyrids meteor shower.

WEST

One of the brightest sights in the sky in recent history, the comet was discovered through photographs by Richard Martin West (b. 1941), a Dane working at the European Southern Observatory.

CARS

In bygone decades, most automobiles used to carry the name of the founder of the marque, and, although plenty of those original names have gone out of business or amalgamated to form new companies, some of the most famous names have survived intact – Ford, Honda, Renault, Porsche, Ferrari, to name a handful.

At various times, eponymous models have been created, as individuals have been honoured by having their name attached to a vehicle. Here are ten automobiles named after a person, rather than a trademarked name.

BLACK MARIA

Maria Lee of Boston, Massachusetts, was a formidable black lady who ran a boarding house in uncompromising fashion back in the 1820s. She apparently rounded up miscreants and delivered them to the police station. When a black police van came on to the scene a few years later, it gained Maria's name.

CADILLAC

Henry Leland, co-founder of the marque which is now owned by General Motors, named the car in honour of his ancestor Antoine Laumet de la Mothe (1658–1730), who called himself 'Sieur de Cadillac' and who helped found Detroit.

DE SOTO

A creation of Walter Chrysler, founder of the eponymous corporation, this model was begun in 1928 and named by Chrysler in honour of Spanish explorer Hernando de Soto (1497–1542), the first European to cross the Mississippi river.

DINO

The Ferrari and Fiat Dino are named after Alfredo 'Dino' Ferrari (1932–56), the son of the Italian firm's founder Enzo. A qualified engineer, Dino was an enthusiastic member of the Ferrari design team and had suggested a V6-engined sports car before he contracted a serious illness and died at the age of just 24. The car was duly christened 'Dino' and the Autodromo Dino Ferrari at Imola was named after him and now bears both his and his father's name.

EDSEL

One of the biggest corporate failures in American automobile history, the Ford Edsel marque was named in honour of Edsel Bryant Ford (1893–1943), the only child of Henry Ford. The Edsel was much hyped but did not sell well and was discontinued in 1960 after just three years' production. Edsel, who succeeded his father in running Ford, deserved a better memorial – he devised the Lincoln Continental (see below), among other makes.

ELISE

The Lotus Elise is a high-class sports car made in England. It is named after Elisa, granddaughter of Romano Artioli, who was chairman of Lotus at the time of its development.

ENZO

The Ferrari Enzo was the most successful limited-edition car ever made. All 400 were pre-sold at prices in excess of £400,000, though the 400th was auctioned for charity and raised nearly £1 million for victims of the 2004 tsunami. They now regularly sell for double their original price.

Enzo Ferrari (1898–1988) founded the eponymous firm after a successful career as a racing driver led him to set up the Ferrari F1 team.

LINCOLN

One of the most famous makes of American automobile, the Lincoln was named by carmaker Henry M Leland after his hero President Abraham Lincoln (1809–65), who has hundreds of other memorials and commemorative items including the State capital of Nebraska.

MERCEDES

Using vehicles supplied by Gottlieb Daimler and Carl Benz, the wealthy Austrian entrepreneur and racing driver Emil Jellinek established a team that he called Mercédès after his young daughter. The brand name caught on as the team swept the boards in motor racing, and the founder officially changed his name to Jellinek-Mercédès. In time, the German manufacturer became Mercedes-Benz.

PICASSO

Marketing and brand experts were looking for a name to signify the Citroën car company's inventiveness, and came up with that of Pablo Ruiz Picasso (1881–1973), the most famous artist of the 20th century. Whether the man himself would have approved of his family's decision to license his name to Citroën is a moot point.

WEAPONS

In factual descriptions and fiction, these weapons have been featured using their name or nickname:

BIG BERTHA

A large-calibre First World War German artillery piece, named after Bertha Krupp (1886–1957) who owned the armaments company for many years. It is also the name of a large-headed driver in golf.

BROWNING

John Browning (1855–1926) invented a range of pistols, shotguns, rifles and machine guns.

COLT

Probably the most famous gun in the world, the .45-calibre, single-action revolver was named after the inventor of revolving pistols, Samuel Colt (1814–62).

DERRINGER

The eponymous single- or two-shot small pistol is wrongly spelled. The inventor's name was American gunsmith Henry Deringer (1768–1868).

GATLING

The predecessor of the machine-gun, the rapid-fire weapon

was invented by Dr Richard J Gatling (1818–1903), an American who believed it would hasten the end of the Civil War.

KALASHNIKOV

The world's most ubiquitous weapon, with 100 million made, the AK-47 or Kalashnikov assault rifle was designed in the Soviet Union by Mikhail Kalashnikov (b. 1919) who later famously said he would rather have invented a lawnmower.

MAXIM

Sir Hiram Maxim (1840–1916) was an American who became a British citizen. He invented the world's first portable automatic machine-gun, as well as a self-reloading mousetrap.

MILLS BOMB

The standard British hand grenade for much of the 20th century was designed by arms manufacturer Sir William Mills (1856–1932). He also designed golf clubs.

MOLOTOV COCKTAIL

The petrol bomb is named after a man who definitely did not want his name associated with it. He was Minister of Foreign Affairs in the Soviet Union Government from 1939 to 1949. The name came from Molotov's claims that the Soviets were sending bread and not bombs to Finland at the start of the war. The Finns, who resorted to petrol bombs for lack of weapons, said their 'cocktails' were to mix with Molotov's bread.

TOMMY GUN

The Thompson sub-machine-gun had several names – the Trench Broom, the Chicago Piano (from its use by gangsters) and its original name, the Annihilator. These were all secondary to the 'Tommy Gun', which came from the name of inventor General John Taliaferro Thompson (1860–1940).

SPORTING TROPHIES

The top ten sports trophies named after people.

DAVIS CUP

In tennis, the international team championship was founded by Dwight Filley Davis (1879–1945) of the USA, originally as a tournament between the USA and Great Britain. He was later the US Secretary of War.

HENRI DELAUNAY TROPHY

The European Football Championship Cup was named in honour of Henri Delaunay (1883–1955) of France, first general secretary of the Union of European Football Associations.

JULES RIMET TROPHY

The original football World Cup was named after Jules Rimet (1873–1956) of France, third president of world governing body FIFA, who devised the tournament. The trophy was won for the third time in 1970 by Brazil and given permanently to them. It was stolen in 1983 and has never been found.

LARRY O'BRIEN TROPHY

The trophy of the NBA Basketball Championship was named in honour of Lawrence Francis O'Brien Jnr (1917–90), former Postmaster General who was Commissioner of the NBA from 1975 to 1984.

RYDER CUP

The trophy of golf's biennial contest between the professionals of the USA and Europe (although originally between Great Britain and Ireland and the USA) was donated by wealthy Englishman Samuel Ryder (1858–1936) who made his fortune in garden seeds and did not play golf until he was 50.

SOLHEIM CUP

The female equivalent of the Ryder Cup was named after Karstein Solheim (1911–2000). He was the American born in Norway who created the PING club brand and campaigned for the tournament.

STANLEY CUP

The trophy for ice hockey's North American National Hockey League Championship was originally donated by Frederick Stanley, 16th Earl of Derby, in 1892 for amateur clubs in Canada where he was then Governor-General.

VINCE LOMBARDI TROPHY

This trophy is presented to the winners of American football's Super Bowl (the world championship game). Vince Lombardi (1913–70) was coach of the Green Bay Packers which won the first two annual championship matches between the winners of the American Football Conference and the National Football Conference. The trophy was renamed after him following his death from cancer. He is revered as the greatest coach in American football history.

WEBB ELLIS CUP

The trophy of the Rugby Union World Cup. With a 'fine disregard' for the rules, William Webb Ellis (1806–72) caught the football and ran with it during a game at Rugby School in Warwickshire. The story is probably apocryphal but, if true, it means that Webb Ellis was cheating – you could not run with the ball. Interesting, given that he became a clergyman.

WIGHTMAN CUP

The prize awarded to the victor of the annual tennis match between the women of the USA and Great Britain. Hazel Hotchkiss Wightman (1886–1974) started it as the female version of the Davis Cup.

Wightman won 17 Grand Slam titles, two Olympic gold medals and had five children, too. America won the trophy so often that the competition was suspended after 1989 and has not been restarted.

CITIES AND TOWNS

There are literally hundreds of cities and towns named after people, real or mythical, across the world. Countries which developed later in history – such as Australia – tend to have more such places than more ancient nations.

Here are some of the best-known eponymous towns and cities and who they are named after.

ADELAIDE, AUSTRALIA
Queen Adelaide (1792–1849), queen consort of King William IV of Great Britain.

ALEXANDRIA, EGYPT
King Alexander III (the Great) of Macedon (356–323BC).

ALICE SPRINGS, AUSTRALIA
Alice Gillan Todd (1836–98), wife of Charles Todd, postmaster general of South Australia.

ATHENS, GREECE
Athena, mythological Greek goddess.

AUCKLAND, NEW ZEALAND
George Eden, 1st Earl of Auckland (1784–1849), Governor-General of India.

BONGOVILLE, GABON
President Omar Bongo (1935–2009). He was born there in what was once a village and is now a sizeable town.

BRAZZAVILLE, CONGO
Pierre Savorgnan de Brazza (1852–1905), Italian-born French explorer.

BRISBANE, AUSTRALIA
Sir Thomas Makdougall Brisbane (1773–1860), Governor of New South Wales.

BUCHAREST, ROMANIA
Bucur, in local legend either a shepherd, prince or fisherman, and most probably an outlaw.

BURY ST EDMUNDS, SUFFOLK, ENGLAND
St Edmund the Martyr (d. 870), King of East Anglia.

COLOGNE (KÖLN), GERMANY
Originally Colonia Agrippina (15–59AD), wife of Emperor Claudius who was born there.

CUIDAD JUAREZ, MEXICO
Benito Juarez (1806–72), Mexican hero, President and reformer.

DARWIN, AUSTRALIA
Charles Robert Darwin (1809–82), naturalist, evolutionist. Originally named Palmerston, the city was designated Darwin in 1911 from the name of its port, which had been named by the commander of *HMS Beagle* in honour of their former shipmate.

DALLAS, USA
George Miffin Dallas (1792–1864), 11th Vice-President of the USA ... or his father or brother, both named Alexander James Dallas.

DURBAN, SOUTH AFRICA
Sir Benjamin d'Urban (1777–1849), Governor of Cape Colony.

FRIEDRICHSHAFEN, GERMANY
King Frederick I (1754–1816), King of Württemberg.

GAGARIN, RUSSIA
Yuri Alekseyevich Gagarin (1934–68), first man in space. Formerly Gzhatsk, renamed in 1968.

GEORGETOWN, GUYANA
King George III (1738–1820), King of Great Britain. The city was previously La Nouvelle Ville and Stabroek, reflecting French and Dutch rule.

GRENOBLE, FRANCE
Emperor Gratian (359–383AD), Roman Emperor who promoted Christianity and was assassinated after a rebellion led by Magnus Maximus.

HALIFAX, NOVA SCOTIA, CANADA
George Montague-Dunk (1716–71), 2nd Earl of Halifax. As First Lord of Trade, he contributed to the foundation of the city.

HAMILTON, ONTARIO, CANADA
George Hamilton (1788–1836), merchant who founded the city.

HOBART, TASMANIA, AUSTRALIA

Robert Hobart (1760–1816), British Secretary of State for War and the Colonies. Originally founded as a penal colony.

HO CHI MINH CITY, VIETNAM

Ho Chi Minh (1890–1969), revolutionary and President of the Democratic Republic of (North) Vietnam. City formerly known as Saigon.

KALININGRAD, RUSSIA

Mikhail Kalinin (1875–1946), chairman of the presidium of the Soviet Union. Formerly Konigsberg, the city is in the enclave separated from the rest of Russia. It was renamed in his honour in the year of his death.

KARLSRUHE, GERMANY

Charles III William (1679–1738), Margrave of Baden-Durlach. He dreamed one night of founding a model city, and did it.

KITCHENER, ONTARIO, CANADA

Field Marshal Herbert Kitchener (1850–1916), 1st Earl Kitchener. The city was known as Berlin from 1854 to 1916, when, with Canada fighting in the First World War, it was renamed after the British Secretary of War who had just been killed at sea.

KRISTIANSAND, NORWAY

King Christian IV (1577–1648), King of Denmark-Norway. He founded the city.

LAS HERAS, MENDOZA, ARGENTINA
Juan Gregorias de Las Heras (1780–1866), Argentine soldier, Governor of Buenos Aires.

LISBON, PORTUGAL
Ulysses (Odysseus), hero of Homer's *Odyssey*. Original name Olissipo.

MELBOURNE, AUSTRALIA
William Lamb (1779–1848), 2nd Viscount Melbourne, Prime Minister of the UK.

MONROVIA, LIBERIA
President James Monroe (1758–1831), fifth President of the USA. He supported the establishment of Liberia.

MUMBAI, INDIA
Mumba (Maha-Amba), the Hindu goddess Mumbadevi.

PAMPLONA, SPAIN
Pompey (Gnaius Pompeius Magnus) (106–48BC). Originally his campsite called Pompaelo.

PORT MORESBY, PAPUA NEW GUINEA
Admiral Sir Fairfax Moresby (1786–1877).

PORT STANLEY, FALKLAND ISLANDS
Edward Smith-Stanley (1799–1869), 14th Earl of Derby, Prime Minister of the UK.

PRETORIA, SOUTH AFRICA
Andries Pretorius (1798–1853), Boer General. His son Marthinus Wessel Pretorius (1819–1901), first president of the South African Republic, founded the city in 1855 and named it after his father and his father's brother.

QUEZON CITY, PHILIPPINES
Manuel Luis Quezon (1878–1944), 2nd President of the Philippines. He developed the city to be capital of the Philippines, but Manila remained the capital.

ROME, ITALY
Romulus, founder of the city with his twin brother Remus. Possibly mythical, definitely legendary, the twins are supposed to have founded the city in the 8th century BC, then Remus died, perhaps at the hands of Romulus who claimed the name for himself.

SAO PAULO, BRAZIL
St Paul (5–67AD), the Apostle of the Gentiles.

SAN FRANCISCO, USA
St Francis of Assisi (1181–1226).

SANTIAGO, CHILE
St James the Apostle.

SEATTLE, USA
Sealth (c.1780–1866), chief of the Duwamish tribe.

SYDNEY, AUSTRALIA
Thomas Townshend (1733–1800), 1st Viscount Sydney. British Home Secretary who encouraged transplantation of convicts.

THESSALONIKI, GREECE
Princess Thessalonike of Macedon (c.350–295BC). Half-sister of Alexander the Great, murdered by her son Antipater II.

VALLETTA, MALTA
Jean Parisot de Valette (1494–1568), Grand Master of the Knights of Malta, who led the defence against the Ottoman Empire in the Great Siege of 1565 and built the city afterwards.

VANCOUVER, CANADA
Captain George Vancouver (1757–98), a Royal Navy officer who served with Captain James Cook and explored the Pacific and the north-west coast of North America. One of the very few people with an island, mountain and city named after him, yet he died in obscurity.

WELLINGTON, NEW ZEALAND
Arthur Wellesley (1769–1852), 1st Duke of Wellington, Prime Minister of the UK.

WILHELMSHAVEN, GERMANY
Emperor Wilhelm (William) I (1797–1888), King of Prussia and German Emperor. He founded the city in 1869.

YEKATERINBURG, RUSSIA

Either after Saint Catherine or Catherine I (1684–1727), Empress of Russia, or both. Formerly known as Sverdlosk, after Yakov Sverdlov, Russian revolutionary leader.

STATES OF THE USA

The ten eponymous States are:

Georgia – King George II of Great Britain (1683–1760)
Louisiana – King Louis XIV of France (1638–1715)
Maryland – Henrietta Maria (1609–69), queen consort of King Charles I of Great Britain
North Carolina – King Charles I of Great Britain (1600–49)
New York – James, then Duke of York and Albany, later King James II of Great Britain (1633–1701)
Pennsylvania – Admiral William Penn (1621–70) (The name was confirmed by King Charles II of Great Britain despite William Penn, son of the Admiral, wanting to call the area simply 'Sylvania', meaning 'wooded territory'.)
South Carolina – King Charles I of Great Britain (1600–49)
Virginia – the Virgin Queen, Elizabeth of England (1533–1603)
Washington – President George Washington
West Virginia – the Virgin Queen, Elizabeth of England (1533–1603)

DOGS

Eleven eponymous breeds:

BOYKIN SPANIEL
Bred by L Whitaker Boykin (1861–1932), who wanted a boat-going Spaniel.

BROHOLMER
Count Nils Frederick Sehested of Broholm, 18th-century Danish breeder. Looks like a cross between a mastiff and a Great Dane.

DANDIE DINMONT
Terrier owned by the eponymous farmer in Sir Walter Scott's novel *Guy Mannering*. Believed to be only breed named after a character in a novel.

DOBERMANN
Bred for the purpose of protection by Karl Friedrich Louis Dobermann (1823–84), with his new 'Pinscher' breed being named posthumously the 'Dobermann Pinscher' by his friends.

GORDON SETTER
Black-and-tan setters predominated in the kennels of Alexander Gordon (1743–1827), 4th Duke of Gordon.

HAMILTONSTÖVARE
The Swedish foxhound, developed in the 19th century by Count Adolf Hamilton, founder of the Swedish Kennel Club.

JACK RUSSELL TERRIER
Reverend John 'Jack' Russell (1795–1883) was known as the

'Sporting Parson' from his love of hunting. He persuaded his milkman to part with his fox terrier bitch, and from her bred dogs which eventually became a separate breed, now known as the various kinds of Russell terrier. Parson Russell helped found the Kennel Club.

KING CHARLES SPANIEL
Though King Charles I of Great Britain kept dogs, his son King Charles II (1630–85) made this particular spaniel popular after the Restoration of the Monarchy in 1660. Individual dogs are recognised in paintings of Charles and his family.

MCNAB COLLIE OR SHEEPDOG
Scottish sheep farmer Alexander McNab brought collies from Scotland to Mendocino in California in the late 19th century, and mated them with existing local sheepdogs to form a new breed.

ST BERNARD
The breed was first described in the 17th century by monks at a hospice in the St Bernard Pass, Switzerland, which had been founded by St Bernard of Menthon (923–1008), also known as Bernard of Montjoux, a Benedictine monk. He is patron saint of the Alps, skiers and snowboarders.

TEDDY ROOSEVELT TERRIER
Like the Teddy Bear, this dog is named after President Theodore Roosevelt (1858–1919), who owned several terriers, but not actually one of the eponymous breed.

INDEX

For those seeking a quick guide to the eponyms within, the following is a list of entries in alphabetical order within each chapter.

Gradgrindian

Gregorian

Herculean

Homeric

Joycean

Jungian

Juvenalian

Kafkaesque

Keynesian

Lucullan

Macabre

Machiavellian

Maudlin

Napeolonic

Nietzschean

Orwellian

Palladian

Pavlovian

Platonic

Promethean

Protean

Pythonesque

Pyrrhic

Quixotic

Rabelaisian

Rubenesque

Runyonesque

Semitic

Shavian

Socratic

Stakhanovite

Stentorian

Stonewall, Stonewaller

Stygian

Tawdry

Terpsichorean

Thespian

Titchy

Victorian

Vitruvian

Wagnerian

Wildean

2. SITE AND SOUND – GEOGRAPHICAL FEATURES

Amundsen Sea

Annapurna

Baffin Island and Bay

Barents Sea

Bering Sea

Brahmaputra River

Dolomites

Doyle's Delight

Gulf of St Lawrence

Hudson Bay

Humboldt Current

Ismoil Somoni Peak

Macgillicuddy's Reeks

Bakelite
Beaufort Scale
Becquerel
Bessemer Process
Biro
Bluetooth
Boolean
Braille
Bunsen Burner
Celsius
Curie
Daguerreotype
Darwinism
Davy Lamp
Decibel
Diesel
Dolby
Doppler Shift or Effect
Fahrenheit
Faraday's Law (and other attributions)
Fibonacci Sequence
Galvanisation, Galvanise
Degauss
Geiger Counter
Heaviside Layer
Hertz; Megahertz
Joule
Kelvin
Listeria

Mach Numbers
Mendelian Genetics or Inheritance
Mercator Projection
Morse Code
Napier's Bones
Neanderthal
Newtonian Laws
Oedipus Complex
Ohm
Pascal
Pythagoras' Theorem
Richter Scale
Roentgen
Sievert
Smithsonian Institution
Venn Diagram
Volt; Voltage (adj. Voltaic)
Watt
Van Allen Belts

MEDICAL ATTRIBUTIONS
Achilles Tendon
Addison's Disease
Alzheimer's
Asperger Syndrome
Bell's Palsy
Bilharzia
Brucellosis
Caesarian Section

Trostkyism

Wesleyan

Zoroastrianism

4. IMMACULATE CONCEPTIONS - DERIVATIONS

Achilles Heel

Beau Brummell

Benedict Arnold

Benny

Bevin Boy

Bluebeard

Bobby

Bowdlerise

Boycott

Botch

Braggadocio

Braidys

Bunkum

Casanova

Churchillian Gesture

Doubting Thomas

Dunce

Eminence Grise

Epicure

Fanny Adams

Foxtrot

Gaia Theory

Hobson's Choice

Hooker

Hooliganism

Jekyll and Hyde

Jezebel

John Hancock

Jonah

Judas

Juggernaut

Lynching

Malapropism

Martinet

Masochism

Maverick

Mentor

Methuselah

Micawber

Midas Touch

Mnemonics

Nemesis

Odyssey

Paparazzi

Pander

Paul Jones (dance)

Pilates

Ponzi Scheme

Quisling

Rachmanism

Rambo

Ritz

5. LAYING DOWN THE LAW - EPONYMOUS LAWS

6. NATURAL SELECTION - EPONYMS IN NATURE

Fuchsia
Guppy
John Dory
Loganberry
McIntosh Apples
Magnolia
Père David's Deer
Poinsettia
Przewalski's Horse
Sequoia
Thomson's Gazelle
Wisteria

7. ALL IN THE BEST POSSIBLE TASTE - EATING RELATED

Albert Pudding
Atkins Diet
Bath Oliver Biscuits
Battenberg Cake
Bechamel Sauce
Beef Wellington
Bismarck Herrings
Caesar Salad
Carpaccio
Celery Victor
Chateaubriand
Chicken à la King
Clementines

Cobb Salad
Crêpe Suzette
Dobos Torte
Dom Perignon
Dr Pepper
Duxelles
Earl Grey Tea
Eggs Benedict
Garibaldi Biscuit
Graham Crackers
Granny Smith Apple
Harvey Wallbanger
Kaiser Rolls
St Honoré Cake
Jules Verne Sauce
Kung Pao chicken
Lamingtons
Margarita
Melba Toast
Mornay Sauce
Omelette Arnold Bennett
Oysters Rockefeller
Pavlova
Peach Melba
Pickles
Pizza Margherita
Pommes Anna
Praline
Queen Mother's Cake
Rumford Soup

8. NAME, SET AND MATCH
- SPORTING EPONYMS